W9-DBE-685

Top Careers in Two Years

Health Care, Medicine, and Science

Titles in the *Top Careers in Two Years* Series

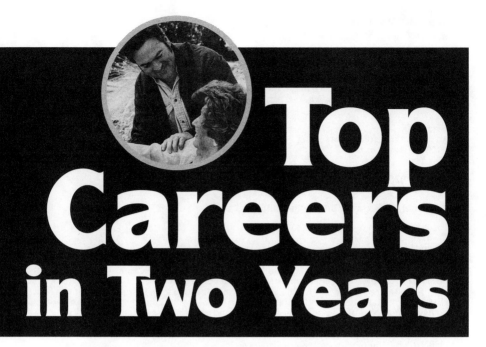

Top Careers in Two Years

Health Care, Medicine, and Science

By Deborah Porterfield

Ferguson Publishing
An imprint of Infobase Publishing

Top Careers in Two Years
Health Care, Medicine, and Science

Ferguson
An imprint of Infobase Publishing
132 West 31st Street
New York, NY 10001

ISBN-13: 978-0-8160-6901-9
ISBN-10: 0-8160-6901-8

Library of Congress Cataloging-in-Publication Data

Top careers in two years.
   v. cm.
   Includes index.
   Contents: v. 1. Food, agriculture, and natural resources / by Scott Gillam — v. 2. Construction and trades / Deborah Porterfield — v. 3. Communications and the arts / Claire Wyckoff — v. 4. Business, finance, and government administration / Celia W. Seupal — v. 5. Education and social services / Jessica Cohn — v. 6. Health care, medicine, and science / Deborah Porterfield — v. 7. Hospitality, human services, and tourism / Rowan Riley — v. 8. Computers and information technology / Claire Wyckoff — v. 9. Public safety, law, and security / Lisa Cornelio, Gail Eisenberg — v. 10. Manufacturing and transportation — v. 11. Retail, marketing, and sales / Paul Stinson.
   ISBN-13: 978-0-8160-6896-8 (v. 1 : hc : alk. paper)
   ISBN-10: 0-8160-6896-8 (v. 1 : hc : alk. paper)
   ISBN-13: 978-0-8160-6897-5 (v. 2 : hc. : alk. paper)
   ISBN-10: 0-8160-6897-6 (v. 2 : hc. : alk. paper)
   ISBN-13: 978-0-8160-6898-2 (v. 3 : hc : alk. paper)
   ISBN-10: 0-8160-6898-4 (v. 3 : hc : alk. paper)
   ISBN-13: 978-0-8160-6899-9 (v. 4 : hc : alk. paper)
   ISBN-10: 0-8160-6899-2 (v. 4 : hc : alk. paper)
   ISBN-13: 978-0-8160-6900-2 (v. 5 : hc : alk. paper)
   ISBN-10: 0-8160-6900-X (v. 5 : hc : alk. paper)
   ISBN-13: 978-0-8160-6901-9 (v. 6 : hc : alk. paper)
   ISBN-10: 0-8160-6901-8 (v. 6 : hc : alk. paper)
   ISBN-13: 978-0-8160-6902-6 (v. 7 : hc : alk. paper)
   ISBN-10: 0-8160-6902-6 (v. 7 : hc : alk. paper)
   ISBN-13: 978-0-8160-6903-3 (v. 8 : hc : alk. paper)
   ISBN-10: 0-8160-6903-4 (v. 8 : hc : alk. paper)
   ISBN-13: 978-0-8160-6904-0 (v. 9 : hc : alk. paper)
   ISBN-10: 0-8160-6904-2 (v. 9 : hc : alk. paper)
   ISBN-13: 978-0-8160-6905-7 (v. 10 : hc : alk. paper)
   ISBN-10: 0-8160-6905-0 (v. 10 : hc : alk. paper)
   ISBN-13: 978-0-8160-6906-4 (v. 11 : hc : alk. paper)
   ISBN-10: 0-8160-6906-9 (v. 11 : hc : alk. paper)
   1. Vocational guidance—United States. 2. Occupations—United States. 3. Professions—United States.
   HF5382.5.U5T677 2007
   331.7020973—dc22

                                                                              2006028638

Produced by Print Matters, Inc.
Text design by A Good Thing, Inc.
Cover design by Salvatore Luongo

Printed in the United States of America

Sheridan PMI 10 9 8 7 6 5 4 3 2 1

This book is printed on acid-free paper.

Contents

How to Use This Book

This book, part of the *Top Careers in Two Years* series, highlights in-demand careers for readers considering a two-year degree program—either straight out of high school or after working a job that does not require advanced education. The focus throughout is on the fastest-growing jobs with the best potential for advancement in the field. Readers learn about future prospects while discovering jobs they may never have heard of.

An associate's degree can be a powerful tool in launching a career. This book tells you how to use it to your advantage, explore job opportunities, and find local degree programs that meet your needs.

Each chapter provides the essential information needed to find not just a job but a career that fits your particular skills and interests. All chapters include the following features:

- "Vital Statistics" provides crucial information at a glance, such as salary range, employment prospects, education or training needed, and work environment.

- Discussion of salary and wages notes hourly versus salaried situations as well as potential benefits. Salary ranges take into account regional differences across the United States.

- "Keys to Success" is a checklist of personal skills and interests needed to thrive in the career.

- "A Typical Day at Work" describes what to expect at a typical day on the job.

- "Two-Year Training" lays out the value of an associate's degree for that career and what you can expect to learn.

- "What to Look For in a School" provides questions to ask and factors to keep in mind when selecting a two-year program.

- "The Future" discusses prospects for the career going forward.

- "Interview with a Professional" presents firsthand information from someone working in the field.

❧ "Job Seeking Tips" offers suggestions on how to meet and work with people in the field, including how to get an internship or apprenticeship.

❧ "Career Connections" lists Web addresses of trade organizations providing more information about the career.

❧ "Associate's Degree Programs" provides a sampling of some of the better-known two-year schools.

❧ "Financial Aid" provides career-specific resources for financial aid.

❧ "Related Careers" lists similar related careers to consider.

In addition to a handy comprehensive index, the back of the book features two appendices providing invaluable information on job hunting and financial aid. Appendix A, Tools for Career Success, provides general tips on interviewing either for a job or two-year program, constructing a strong résumé, and gathering professional references. Appendix B, Financial Aid, introduces the process of applying for aid and includes information about potential sources of aid, who qualifies, how to prepare an application, and much more.

Introduction

Workers who choose a health career often do so for altruistic reasons: Quite simply, they want to help others. Whether it's a licensed practical nurse attending to a surgery patient or a dental hygienist cleaning a child's teeth, health care workers take great satisfaction in knowing they make a difference in people's lives.

In fact, according to the U.S. Bureau of Labor Statistics, eight of the 20 fastest growing occupations will be in the health care field. Specifically, between 2004 and 2014, employment opportunities will increase by:

✔ 55 percent for physician assistants
✔ 54 percent for medical assistants
✔ 44 percent for dental hygienists
✔ 41 percent for physical therapist assistants and aides
✔ 30 percent for medical records technicians

Credit the aging population for much of the expected boom in health care. As people grow older, they typically require more medical care, thus creating a demand for health care workers. Advances in medical technology also are creating new positions for health care specialists who help identify and treat conditions that used to be untreatable. Plus, pressures to contain medical costs will create new opportunities for support workers, such as medical assistants, surgical technologists, speech-language pathology assistants, and pharmacy technicians.

Because employers must scramble to fill positions, they often try to lure skilled health care workers with valuable fringe benefits. Many health care providers, for example, reimburse employees who continue their educational training, while others provide family-friendly benefits such as childcare services and flexible schedules.

In this volume, you'll learn about the many rewarding careers in the health field that have shown the most potential for growth in the near future. While the job descriptions may vary, the workers who hold these jobs all share one common goal: improving the health care of their patients. Depending on the job, the care provided may be dramatic, such as when a surgical technologist helps resuscitate a patient in cardiac arrest. The care can also be given indirectly, such as when a medical records technician fast-tracks paperwork so a worried patient can schedule a biopsy sooner rather than later.

No matter what their job titles are, health care providers must be able to work together as a team: A pharmacy technician must share information with doctors, nurses, and insurance specialists to ensure that patients get the medicine they need; and a licensed practical nurse must leave clear notes when updating a patient's chart, so doctors and other nurses readily comprehend the patient's status.

Beyond Blood and Guts

Of course, not everyone has the disposition needed to deal with life-and-death situations, not to mention the sight of blood and open wounds; but the good news is that not all health careers require a strong stomach, or, in some cases, even direct contact with patients.

For example, a medical records technician spends much of his or her day on a computer, making sure patients' records are complete and accurate, while a pharmacy technician works behind the counter, preparing prescriptions for patients.

Other health care professionals work as therapists, or teachers, who help patients achieve specific goals. A physical therapist assistant, for instance, teaches patients to perform exercises that improve their ability to perform basic tasks, such as walking and standing.

Some health care workers also work in sales. Dispensing opticians don't just help fit customers with prescription glasses, but also sell them. Likewise, pharmacy technicians sometimes help out at the register, ringing up prescriptions and other drugstore goods.

Some health care workers don't actually take care of people: They attend special schools where they are trained to take care of dogs, cats, horses, and other animals.

As you would expect, most health care employees work inside medical facilities, such as doctor's offices, health care centers, and hospitals. There are exceptions, however. Health care workers such as dialysis technicians and licensed practical nurses sometimes provide care in patients' homes.

We could only include a sampling of health careers in this volume. Others you might want to explore include occupational therapy assistant, medical transcriptionist, respiratory therapist, cardiology technician, and radiology technician.

Even though the job descriptions for the different health careers vary, all require some common skills. Whether you're a nurse giving a patient a shot or a dialysis technician setting up the machinery, you need to be a careful, conscientious worker who can be counted on to worry about the details. You also need to be a good communicator who can share vital medical information with other health care providers, patients, and patients' families.

Most important, you need to be a special kind of person who can be compassionate, yet not become so involved in a patient's well-being that you let your emotions affect your health and good judgment.

Benefits of an Associate's Degree

When people think about the medical profession, many mistakenly assume that most jobs require years of advanced training. While it's certainly true that doctors, dentists, and similar professionals require advanced degrees, many rewarding health careers are available to those who earn an associate's degree at an accredited community college, trade school, or technical school.

In fact, most of the new health jobs that will be created in the next few years will require less than four years of college, opening up opportunities for students who enroll in two-year health care programs. Not only do these schools cost less money and require a smaller time commitment than traditional four-year schools, but also their programs often focus on helping students gain the skills they need to work in rewarding careers.

The time and effort needed to earn an associate's degree can produce tangible rewards: Students who earn an associate's degree tend to make $2,000 to $6,000 a year more than those who try to get by with just a high school diploma.

For many students, the lower costs of community colleges play a key role in their decision about which school to choose. The average annual tuition and fees for attending a four-year public school in a student's home state was about $5,130 during the 2004–2005 school year, while the tuition to attend a community college was about $2,080, according to a survey by the College Board. Students who attend schools away from home must also pay room and board fees, which at state schools increases the average tally to about $11,350 a year.

Students who struggle in high school find an open door at community colleges, which accept those with less than stellar grade point averages and SAT scores. Plus, such schools frequently provide special classes and tutors who can help students strengthen basic skills; and because the class sizes at community schools are typically smaller than those at universities, students often receive more personalized instruction.

Two-year schools also provide flexible scheduling, which can make it easier for some students to attend. Students who work during the day, for example, can often take classes at night. Those who attend a school nearby can save money by living at home; and at some schools, students can even take courses online.

At a community college, you can enroll in a program leading to an associate's degree in arts or science (A.A. or A.S.) or in applied science (A.A.S.). To earn an A.A.S., you usually take specialized courses in fields such as construction technology, medical assisting, or electronics, as well as general education courses in subjects such as English and math. These degrees take about two years to complete.

During your two years of study, you'll take a mix of general college classes and career-based courses that will train you to work in your chosen career, whether licensed practical nurse, physical therapist assistant, or speech therapy assistant.

Many health programs also require students to work as interns or trainees under the supervision of a trained health care provider. For example, to earn an associate's degree in the speech-language pathology assistant program at Pasadena City College in California, you must complete supervised clinical fieldwork in a public school and a medical facility, such as a hospital or clinic. Such valuable on-the-job training helps you gain real-life experience under the watchful eye of an experienced professional.

If you have your heart set on working in the health field but don't want to pursue a two-year degree, some college programs award certificates to students who complete courses directly related to their chosen profession. For example, you can enroll in classes that lead to certificates in specialties such as emergency medicine or dialysis. These programs typically take six months to a year to complete.

Is a Health Career Right for You?

Ask yourself the following questions to see if the careers in this book might be right for you.

✔ Do you enjoy helping others?

✔ Can you handle pressure?

✔ Are you a problem solver?

✔ Are you a team player who can take direction from others?

✔ Are you a conscientious worker?

✔ Are you good with details?

✔ Do you have solid math skills?

✔ Are you emotionally stable enough to handle life-and-death situations?

✔ If you'll be caring for patients, can you handle the sight of blood and other bodily fluids?

✔ Are you dependable? (You've missed very few days of school or work.)

✔ Can you get along with different personalities?

✔ Do you like variety in your work?

✔ Do you enjoy science?

✔ Are you interested in how the body works?

✔ Are you a quick thinker?

✔ Are you flexible about your work schedules? (Would you be willing to work weekends or nights?)

If you answered yes to most of these, then a health career might be for you.

Finding the Right School

A good place to start your search for a two-year college that fits your needs is http://www.collegeboard.com. You can key in specific criteria, such as the program you want to study or the area where you want to live, and it'll display options that meet your needs. You also can find information about colleges at libraries, which usually have college directories and individual catalogues. When you find a college that interests you, check out its Web site, look over its catalogue, and talk to someone at the school. If the school is nearby, you may even want to visit its campus to get a feel for the place.

When choosing a school, look for one that's accredited by professional associations in your field. Unfortunately, some so-called "diploma mills" run fraudulent programs: They hand out worthless diplomas and certificates without teaching students the skills they need to work in their chosen professions. To learn more about such fraudulent schools, check "Diploma Mills and Accreditation" at the U.S. Department of Education's Web site: http://www.ed.gov/students/prep/college/diplomamills/index.html. The Council for Higher Education Accreditation also offers helpful information at http://www.chea.org.

The best way to avoid such pitfalls is to enroll in accredited schools and programs. The following are top accrediting agencies for schools:

Accrediting Council for Independent Colleges and Schools
http://www.acics.org

Distance Education and Training Council
http://www.detc.org

Middle States Association of Colleges and Schools
http://www.msacs.org

New England Association of Schools and Colleges
http://www.neasc.org/

North Central Association of Colleges and Schools
http://www.ncahigherlearningcommission.org/

Northwest Association of Schools and Colleges
http://www.opi.state.mt.us/nascu/text.htm

Southern Association of Colleges and Schools
http://www.sacs.org

Western Association of Schools and Colleges
http://www.wascweb.org/

Plus, many professional health organizations offer accreditation and certification for specific health programs. They include:

Accreditation Review Committee on Education in Surgical Technology http://www.arcst.org

Commission on Accreditation of Allied Health Education Programs http://www.caahep.org/

Commission on Accreditation for Health Informatics and Information Management Education http://www.cahiim.org

Accrediting Bureau of Health Education Schools http://www.abhes.org

Accrediting Commission of the National Association of Trade and Technical Schools http://www.accsct.org

American Academy of Physician Assistants http://www.aapa.org

American Veterinary Medical Association http://www.avma.org

Commission on Accreditation in Physical Therapy Education http://www.apta.org

Commission on Dental Accreditation http://ada.org/prof/ed/accred/commission/index.asp

Commission on Opticianry Accreditation http://www. coaccreditation.com

Committee on Accreditation for EMS Professionals http://www.coaemsp.org

National Council of State Boards of Nursing http://www.ncsbn.org

National League for Nursing Accrediting Commission http://www.nlnac.org

If you think there's a chance you might want to continue your schooling, make sure that most of the credits earned in the two-year program can be transferred to a four-year school. Someone with training as a medical assistant, for example, can continue his or her training to become a physician's assistant with more responsibility and a higher paycheck. Likewise, a veterinarian technician may decide to go back to school to become a veterinarian technologist, which generally requires four years of school. The good news is that once you start working in the health field, employers will often help pay for additional schooling.

Health Contacts

For general information on health careers, contact:

American Medical Association/Health Professions Career and Education Directory
515 N. State Street
Chicago, IL 60610
http://www.ama-assn.org/go/alliedhealth

Bureau of Health Professions
Parklawn Room 8A-09
5600 Fishers Lane
Rockville, MD 20857
http://www.bhpr.hrsa.gov

Dental Hygienist/ Dental Assistant

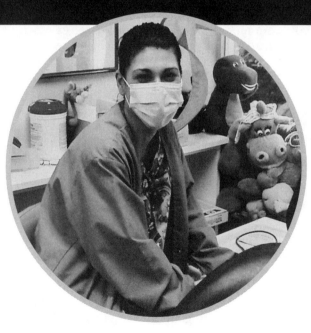

> ## Vital Statistics
>
> **Salary:** The median wage for dental hygienists is about $28 an hour, or more than $58,000 a year; and the median wage for dental assistants is about $13.60 an hour, or more than $28,000 a year, according to 2006 figures from the U.S. Bureau of Labor Statistics.
>
> **Employment:** The demand for skilled dental hygienists and dental assistants is excellent and is expected to continue to grow.
>
> **Education:** Accredited schools provide essential training and instruction for people who want to pursue a career in the dental field.
>
> **Work Environment:** Dental hygienists and dental assistants work in well-lit dental offices and often are able to create flexible work schedules. Dental hygienists and assistants wear protective masks, safety glasses, and gloves while they work with patients.

Do you have a dazzling smile? Your dental hygienist deserves much of the credit. When you visit the dental office, dental hygienists are the ones who make your teeth sparkle. Their job goes well beyond just saying, "Please spit in this sink." Using special dental tools, they remove stains and plaque from your teeth. They examine your teeth and gums, making notes of any problems. Depending on what needs to be done, a dental hygienist may also take X-rays of your teeth, give you a fluoride treatment, or help the dentist fill a cavity. If you need to do a better job brushing or flossing, a dental hygienist will show you how.

Dental assistants also play an important role in keeping your teeth in good shape. Besides offering advice on dental care, they often assist the dentist while she or he works. They hand tools to the dentist, and hold devices—such as suction tools—in a patient's mouth. They prepare the dental instruments and help remove sutures.

The key difference in assistants and hygienists is that dental hygienists are licensed to perform more clinical tasks. Consequently, hygienists typically earn more. Among dental hygienists, top earners make about $41 an hour, whereas the best-paid dental assistants make about $20 an hour.

Enrolling in an associate's degree program approved by the Commission on Dental Accreditation can help prepare you for a career as a dental hygienist or dental assistant. To become a registered dental hygienist, you'll need to pass a national written exam administered by the American Dental Association's Joint Commission on National Dental Examinations and a clinical exam given by a state or regional agency.

Students enrolled in dental assistant programs can complete their training in as little as one year, or pursue a two-year degree. While the specific requirements for dental assistants vary from state to state, most require dental assistants to be licensed or registered by the state board. Even though certification by the Dental Assisting Board is voluntary in some states, dental assistants who take the time to pass the national exam often land better-paying jobs.

Dental hygienists hold about 158,000 jobs in the United States, while dental assistants hold about 267,000. One of the attractions for many workers is the profession's flexibility. More than half of all dental hygienists work fewer than 35 hours a week, giving them time to care for families or pursue other interests. Dental assistants also often work part time, sometimes splitting their duties between different dental offices.

Because dental health affects your overall well-being, dental hygienists and assistants take pride in knowing that they help keep a patient's teeth—and entire body—in good health.

> ## "You don't have to brush your teeth— just the ones you want to keep."
> ### —Author unknown

On the Job

Dental hygienists play a vital role in a dentist's office. They look over a patient's teeth and gums, and write notes about any problems they spot. Working with various dental instruments, they then clean, polish, and floss a patient's teeth. Depending on what the patient needs, they may take and develop X-rays of the teeth, apply fluoride treatments, or smooth metal restorations.

During an office visit, a hygienist will often offer helpful suggestions on dental care. One patient, for example, may be told to switch to a softer brush, while another might be shown a better flossing technique. Dental assistants also help care for patients in a dental office. They often work next to the dentist, handing over instruments or holding a suction device in a patient's mouth. Tasks vary from office to office, and they are often dependent on an assistant's training. Some dental assistants make casts of the teeth and temporary crowns, take dental X-rays, and remove sutures. Others run the office: They schedule appointments, handle payments, pay office bills, and order dental supplies.

Keys to Success

To be a successful dental hygienist or dental assistant, you need

- manual dexterity
- good communication skills
- excellent hand-eye coordination
- thoroughness
- a reassuring, soothing manner
- attention to detail
- people skills

Do You Have What It Takes?

To be a dental hygienist or assistant, you need to work well with people. Because you're often doing intricate work inside a patient's mouth, you must possess excellent fine motor skills and outstanding hand-eye coordination. Teaching patients how to maintain healthy dental habits is a big part of the job, so knowing how to communicate with others is vital.

A Typical Day at Work

Dental hygienists and dental assistants work in dental offices, schools, health clinics, nursing homes, and other medical settings. Many work part time and have flexible schedules that let them choose which days and hours they work.

Not only do dental hygienists clean and examine a patient's teeth, but also they teach patients how to take better care of their teeth. At the beginning of the day, dental hygienists and dental assistants look over the day's schedule, check the patients' charts, and ready supplies for the day. When a patient arrives, the hygienist seats the patient, asks about his or her health, and examines the patient's teeth and gums. Depending on what a patient needs, a hygienist or assistant will take and develop X-rays of the teeth, assist a dentist while he or she fills in a cavity, or show a patient a better brushing technique.

How to Break In

You can get a jump on a career as a dental assistant or dental hygienist in high school by taking related courses, such as biology, chemistry, and office management. While in college, be sure to reach out to the local chapters of the American Dental Hygienists' Association (ADHA) or American Dental Assistant Association (ADAA). Doing so will give you a chance to find a mentor, who can advise you on college choices, internships, and other career topics. Your mentor may even be able to arrange for you spend a day with a dental hygienist or assistant, so you can see what a typical day is like.

Two-Year Training

Enrolling in a two-year accredited program can prepare you to become a licensed dental hygienist. The Commission on Dental Accreditation has approved more than 260 programs, so you'll have plenty from which to choose. During school, you'll have a chance to take traditional college courses, such as chemistry, microbiology, physiology, and social sciences, as well as subjects tied to dentistry, including gum disease, radiology, and clinical dental hygiene.

Most states require dental hygienists to be licensed. To be licensed, you'll typically need to earn an associate's degree from an accredited program, pass a national exam, and complete a regional or state clinical board exam. Dental assistant students receive instruction in classrooms and have opportunities to gain real-life experience in dental schools, clinics, and dental offices.

Even though national certification is voluntary in some states, taking the time to pass certification exams administered by the Dental Assisting National Board (DANB) shows potential employers that you have mastered the skills needed to do the job and take your career seriously.

What to Look For in a School

When considering a two-year school, be sure to ask these questions:

☞ Does the school offer coursework that teaches you how to work with dental patients, dental equipment, and dental records?

☞ What is the school's job placement rate?

☞ What are the instructors' credentials? Have they worked in the industry?

☞ Will the school prepare you to take and pass certification exams in your field?

☞ Is the program accredited by the Commission on Dental Accreditation?

☞ If there's a chance you might want to continue your schooling at a later date, can the credits be applied to the pursuit of a bachelor's degree?

The Future

The demand for skilled dental hygienists and dental assistants is expected to be strong with the job growth exceeding that of other occupations, according to the U.S. Bureau of Labor Statistics. One reason? Not only are people living longer, but many more are keeping their teeth, requiring an increase in dental care.

Interview with a Professional:
Q & A

Margaret Lappan Green
Registered dental hygienist, Newport News, Virginia;
and adjunct professor, Old Dominion University,
School of Dental Hygiene, Norfolk, Virginia

Q: *How did you get started?*

A: My father was a medical illustrator/medical photographer at a hospital, and he was the one who said, "Here, go check out this dental hygienist program." He dropped me off at a children's hospital in Pittsburgh for the entire day. I had a chance to scrub up and go into a surgery with a couple of dentists doing full mouth reconstruction. I was amazed that one could help someone that way.

I saw a hygienist talking to a patient. She was helping people like a nurse. My father explained how I could do a dental hygienist curriculum at the University of Pittsburgh. I applied for it and was accepted. And I've never been happier since that day. It's a fabulous career. I always saw my parents helping other people, so being a dental hygienist was an automatic fit.

Q: *What's a typical day like?*

A: As a practicing clinician, I start off the day reviewing the charts of the patients I'll be seeing that day. I've allotted every hour for every patient I work with. I first take a medical history and then start with an oral cancer exam. After the oral exam, I look at the teeth to see if there are any problems with the fillings. I look at X-rays. I look at the gum tissue.

I have a chair-side assistant who helps me. Before I see a patient, the assistant takes a patient's blood pressure. Then we use a pink staining solution that reveals invisible plaque. All my patients are supposed to come in, having already brushed their teeth. I might go over brushing and show them other dental tools. I spend a lot of time on education.

As I'm doing the exam, I have a dental assistant who records findings, so when the doctor comes around to see a patient, I've already collected the data. Based on that assessment, I plan out the treatment. It could be preventive. If you have a child who has a higher risk for decay, you may decide to do a fluoride varnish rather than just a topical treatment of fluoride.

I will see about eight patients a day. We are booking 45-minute to one-hour appointments. You need that time to educate and develop rapport with your patients.

When I'm done, I do dictation on all the patients I saw. A hygienist is responsible as a licensed provider of care to document what she does.

Q: *What's your advice for those starting a career?*

A: First of all, you need very good study skills. The curriculum is 80 to 85 percent science. Take a lot of science and math in high school. You have to enjoy working with people.

I would go shadow a dental hygienist. I would observe the hygienist to see the whole picture, to see if you really would be interested in working in that job. Contact the ADHA. They can put you in touch with someone in the local community that you can go and observe. Basically, you're looking for a mentor.

There is a lot of upward mobility for someone pursuing a dental hygiene career. You can come into the career with an associate's degree, but you can continue your education. We can pursue five different roles (a clinician, an educator, a researcher, an administrator, and a public health advocate) in our careers. That's one reason we see such longevity in the profession.

Q: *What's the best part about being a dental hygienist?*

A: The variety that I've been afforded in my career as a dental hygienist. I've grown with every little opportunity that I've taken. No matter what I've done, it seems to make a difference. It may be in a small way but I can go back and feel really good about how I've spent my life.

Did You Know?

The residents of San Salvador, El Salvador, surely had the cleanest teeth in the world on November 5, 2005. That's when 13,380 people brushed their teeth at the same time inside Cuscatla'n Stadium. Organized by Colgate Palmolive, the event is listed as an "amazing feat" in Guinness World Records.

Job Seeking Tips

See the suggestions below and turn to Appendix A for tips on creating a résumé, interviewing for schools or jobs, and collecting references.

✔ Become certified in your specialty.

✔ Decide what you're interested in and seek relevant experience.

✔ Seek advice from the career placement office.

✔ Reach out to associations in your field.

Career Connections

For further information, contact the following organizations.

Academy of General Dentistry http://www.agd.org

American Dental Assistants Association http://www.dental assistant.org

American Dental Hygienists' Association http://www.adha.org

American Dental Association http://www.ada.org

Dental Jobs at Dental Workers.com http://www.dentalworkers.com

Associate's Degree Programs

Here are a few schools offering quality dental programs:

Baltimore City Community College, Baltimore, Maryland

Carl Sandburg College, Galesburg, Illinois

Laramie County Community College, Laramie, Wyoming

Fones School of Dental Hygiene, University of Bridgeport, Bridgeport, Connecticut

Monroe Community College, Rochester, New York

Johnson County Community College, Overland Park, Kansas

Financial Aid

Here is one dental scholarship to get you started. For more on financial aid for two-year students, turn to Appendix B.

The **American Dental Hygienists' Association** offers scholarships to those who meet one of several requirements, such as being a minority student or showing leadership potential. Member students enrolled in an accredited dental hygiene program are eligible for the ADHA Institute for Oral Health scholarship.   http://www.adha.org/

Related Careers

Medical assistant, occupational therapist assistant, occupational therapist aide, physical therapist assistant, physical therapist aide, and physician assistant.

Dispensing Optician

Vital Statistics

Salary: The median annual salary for dispensing opticians is about $28,000, according to 2006 data from the U.S. Bureau of Labor Statistics.

Employment: The demand for certified dispensing opticians is high and is expected to continue to grow.

Education: Accredited schools and apprenticeship programs provide essential instruction for people who want to work as dispensing opticians.

Work Environment: Opticians work in hospitals, clinics, optical chain stores, and medical offices.

If you need new prescription glasses, a dispensing optician can help you find just the right pair. Commonly referred to as opticians, these skilled workers are licensed to adapt and fit corrective glasses based on a prescription written by an optometrist. Some opticians also are licensed to work with contact lenses.

When a customer comes in with a prescription for eyeglasses, an optician helps him or her select frames that suit the customer's face and personal style. Once the customer has selected the frames, the optician writes an order for the glasses that specifies the selected frames and the prescriptive lenses. An ophthalmic lab tech, or in some cases, the optician, then uses the order's specifications to grind and insert the lenses into the selected frame.

When the eyeglasses are ready, the optician helps the customer try on the new glasses, and makes any adjustments needed for a good fit. The optician also gives the customer tips on wearing and caring for the glasses.

Taking optician courses at a community college or tech school while working as an apprentice will give you the skills needed to work as an optician. The college courses will help you understand your field while the on-the-job training will give you essential hands-on experience.

Licensing requirements for opticians vary from state to state. Depending on where you live, you may need to pass a state or national exam, complete an apprenticeship, or earn certification from the American Board of Opticianry (ABO) and/or the National Contact Lens Examiners (NCLE). To keep your license current, some states also require opticians to continue their educational training.

About 66,000 opticians work in the United States. Of these, about 30 percent work in health stores, optician stores, and other personal care stores. Another one-third work in medical offices, including optometry offices. Some opticians work in department stores, warehouse clubs, and other large venues, while others run their own businesses. Top earners in the field make more than $45,300 a year.

An optician's main job is to make sure the customer's prescription is filled correctly; but seasoned opticians with fashion savvy and good communication skills do much more. Consider the anxious child who needs his or her first pair of reading glasses. A skilled optician will talk up the idea of glasses while helping the child find a cool-looking pair that will turn that worried frown into an "I can't-wait to-show-off-my-new-glasses" grin.

On the Job

A skilled optician helps customers select glasses and frames that fit and flatter their faces. To make sure the prescription is filled correctly, the optician measures the distance between the centers of a customer's pupils and the distance between the ocular surface and the lens. If a customer doesn't have a new prescription, the optician can remake the eyeglasses from old prescription records or use a *focimeter* to record the eyeglass measurements on a current pair. The optician then prepares a work order, so the technicians can make the lenses and put them into the right frame.

Once the glasses are ready, the optician checks to make sure they've been ground to the correct specifications. The optician may also use his or her hands or pliers to bend or reshape the frames to fit a patient's face.

Some opticians are trained to fit customers with contact lenses. To fit the lenses, the optician measures the shape and size of the eye. He helps the customer select the best type of contact lens material, and then prepares a work order for the lenses. To fit a patient with contact lenses, an optician carefully observes the patient's eyes, corneas, and lids while working with special instruments and microscopes. During follow-up visits, the optician teaches the customer how to insert, remove, and care for the lenses, and makes sure the fitting is correct.

Keys to Success

To be a successful dispensing optician, you need
- math ability
- tact
- communication skills
- attention to details
- technical savvy
- manual dexterity
- knowledge of physics and geometry
- people skills

Do You Have What It Takes?

To work as a dispensing optician, you need to be a good reader of people. You need to quickly size up a customer's personality, style, and needs and then help the customer pick lenses and frames that he or she will want to wear. Because precision is key when measuring frames and placing orders, attention to details and strong math skills are vital.

A Typical Day at Work

Opticians work in well-lit, comfortable spaces inside medical offices and stores. Their hours may vary, depending on where they work. Those who work for large retailers, for example, sometimes work weekends and nights. Like many retail workers, opticians spend much of their day standing and dealing with a steady stream of customers. At quieter moments, opticians take care of paperwork, such as going over bills.

How to Break In

You can gain valuable experience working at businesses that provide optical services. Whether you start off as a sales clerk or work in a formal apprenticeship program, you'll pick up important job skills and make key contacts in the industry.

While in school, you can become a member of professional organizations, such as the Opticians Association of America. Doing so will provide you with helpful information on jobs, scholarships, and seminars. It also will give you a chance to meet others in your field.

When you finish the required training, take the time to gain certification in your field. The American Board of Opticianry certifies those who dispense and work with spectacles, while the National Contact Lens Examiners certifies those who work with contact lenses. Certification from one or both of these organizations shows prospective employers that you take your career seriously and have obtained the skills needed to do a good job.

Two-Year Training

Enrolling in an accredited optician program can help you get started on the right career path. Some programs can be completed in as little as one year, while some programs last about two years and result in an associate's degree.

During school, you'll learn how to adapt and fit corrective eyewear. You'll learn how to help patients select frames and how to write work orders for lab techs. You'll learn how to measure faces for fitting, and how to adjust and repair frames. You'll be shown how to set up appointments, keep payrolls, and make sales.

You'll have a chance to put this knowledge to work in a formal apprenticeship at a large firm or in an informal learn-as-you-work program at a small business. As an apprentice, you'll gain hands-on experience, working with customers as you adjust glasses, place orders, and make sales under the supervision of a seasoned pro.

Licensing requirements vary from state to state. Some states require you to complete apprenticeship programs, and pass state or national certification exams. Even if it's not required in your state, earning certification from the American Board of Optometry and/or the National Contact Lens Examiners shows potential employers that you've acquired the skills needed to work as an optician.

To ensure that opticians keep up with the ever-changing industry, many states also require proof of continued education for license renewal.

"You go to school, you get a master's degree, you study Shakespeare, and you wind up being famous for plastic glasses."
—Sally Jessy Raphael, television personality

What to Look For in a School

When considering a two-year school, be sure to ask these questions:

☞ Does the school offer work-related courses that teach the basics of your field?

☞ Is the school a member of the National Federation of Opticianry Schools and/or is it accredited by the Commission on Opticianry Accreditation?

☞ Does the school have contacts to help students become apprentices?

☞ What is the school's job placement rate?

☞ Will the program prepare you to take and pass state and/or national certification exams in your field?

☞ What are the instructors' credentials? Have they worked in the industry? Have they kept up with new techniques and procedures in the industry? Are they available outside the classroom?

☞ Do the classrooms and labs have up-to-date equipment?

Interview with a Professional:
Q&A
Tom Graves
President, Schaff Opticians, Greenfield, Massachusetts

Q: *How did you get started?*

A: Actually, I was going to do something in optics and was transferring colleges when I got drafted and I ended up going through the army's [optician] school.

I had some family members involved in the business. I had a job waiting for me when I got out. My older cousin originally owned the business and I went to work for him.

Q: *What's a typical day like?*

A: You do a little bit of everything. I fit contact lens. I teach people how to put them on. We fit glasses, and grind the lenses for the fames, and choose the proper-fitting frames.

For me, I'm usually here a little after 8 in the morning. Basically, in the morning you get ready to go. The contact lens patients are done by appointment. For eyeglasses, they walk in the door. No appointment necessary.

Q: *What's your advice for those starting a career?*

A: There are basically two routes you can go. You can go to an accredited college; there are several scattered throughout the country. The other alternative is to do it through an apprenticeship.

If you're going to work in the retail end, you need good people skills. You need a reasonably solid math background. A little bit of physics and geometry helps. You need good hands skills, as far as assembling the glasses.

Q: *What's the best part about being an optician?*

A: Helping people see. There are some people who really need exotic eyewear to see properly. We know what's available and can sometimes help someone who has almost no vision see again. Some vision problems can only be cured through contact lenses and that can be rewarding.

The Future

As the baby boomers continue to age, so do their eyes, creating a big demand for corrective glasses and lenses. The growing popularity of laser surgery to correct vision problems could eventually curb the demand for eyewear, but for now, the surgery remains too expensive for many people.

Did You Know?

In 1508, Leonardo da Vinci illustrated the concept of contact lenses. Several hundred years later, in 1887, the first manufactured contact lens was made from glass and covered the entire eye.

Job Seeking Tips

See the suggestions below and turn to Appendix A for advice on résumés, and interviews.

✔ Become certified in your area of expertise.

✔ Decide what you're interested in and seek relevant experience.

✔ Seek advice from the career placement office.

✔ Reach out to associations in your chosen field.

Career Connections

For further information, contact the following organizations.

American Board of Opticianry http://www.abo.org

Commission on Opticianry Accreditation http://www.coaccreditation.com

The International Society for Optical Engineering http://www.spie.org

National Academy of Opticianry http://www.nao.org

National Federation of Opticianry Schools http://www.nfos.org

Optical Society of America (OSA) http://www.osa.org

Opticians Association of America (OAA) http://www.oaa.org

Associate's Degree Programs

Here are a few schools offering quality dispensing optician programs:

East Mississippi Community College, Scooba, Mississippi

Hillsborough Community College, Tampa, Florida

Indiana University, School of Optometry, Bloomington, Indiana

Erie Community College, Buffalo, New York

Financial Aid

Here are a couple optician-related scholarships. For more on financial aid for two-year students, turn to Appendix B.

The **International Society for Optical Engineering** awards scholarships to student members who are enrolled or plan to enroll full-time in an optics, imaging, photonics, and similar programs. http://www.spie.org

The **Robert G. Corns, O.D. Scholarship** goes to students in their second year of study in an optician/technician program at the University of Indiana.   http://www.opt.indiana.edu/programs/opttech/corns_app.doc

Related Careers

Jeweler, precious stone worker, metal worker, locksmith, orthodontist, prosthetist, and precision instrument repair worker.

Physical Therapist Assistant/ Physical Therapist Aide

Vital Statistics

Salary: The median salary for physical therapist assistants (PTAs) is about $38,000 a year, according to 2006 data from the U.S. Bureau of Labor Statistics. The bureau reports median salary for physical therapist aides as about $21,400.

Employment: An aging baby boom population is expected to fuel the need for physical therapist assistants and physical therapist aides.

Education: Accredited schools can provide essential instruction and training for people who want to work as physical therapist assistants. On-the-job training is generally required for those pursuing work as physical therapist aides.

Work Environment: Depending on the assignment, a physical therapist assistant or physical therapist aide may work in a hospital, rehab clinic, physical therapy office, or in a patient's home.

Physical therapy plays a vital role in keeping people mobile. When a skier breaks a leg, a doctor puts on the cast, but it's the physical therapist— and often the physical therapist assistant—who helps the patient walk again. Under the direction of physical therapists, physical therapist assistants help improve the quality of life for patients who suffer from lower-back pain, arthritis, cerebral palsy, and other disabling conditions. Depending on the patient's needs, they perform massages or apply heat packs to ease the pain. In some cases, they help the patient perform exercises to strengthen muscles that have been weakened from disease or a fracture.

Physical therapist aides also pitch in, organizing a patient's treatment tools; helping a patient walk to a treatment area; and handling appointment calls, billing, and other clerical duties.

Physical therapist aides often receive their training on the job, while physical therapist assistants generally receive their training through a two-year degree program that combines classroom instruction with clinical rotations.

About 59,000 physical therapist assistants and 43,000 physical therapist aides work in the United States. Of those, about 60 percent work in hospitals and physical therapy offices. Others work in nursing care facilities, physicians' offices, and outpatient care centers, as well as for home health care services.

Experienced physical therapist assistants are well paid, with the top 10 percent making more than $52,000. Physical therapist aides, who aren't required to have formal training, make less, with top earners making more than $33,500 a year.

Making a decent salary is, of course, an important factor in choosing a career; but for many physical therapist assistants and aides, the true reward comes from helping a patient become independent. Whether it's helping a stroke victim learn to walk again or teaching a struggling toddler to sit on his or her own, the satisfaction of knowing you've made a difference in someone's life can be priceless.

On the Job

A physical therapist assistant works under the supervision of a physical therapist. In this role, you may be asked to help patients do strength-building exercises, or give them pain-relieving massages, paraffin baths, and hot or cold pack treatments. While you work, you'll record the patient's responses to the various treatments, so you can share your observations with the physical therapist.

A physical therapist aide also works under the supervision of a physical therapist, or in some cases, under the direction of a physical therapist assistant. As a physical therapist aide, your job is to clean and organize the treatment area so it's ready for the next patient. If a patient has trouble walking, you may be asked to help move him or her to the treatment area. You may also answer the phone, order supplies, fill out insurance forms, and perform other clerical duties.

Keys to Success

To be a successful physical assistant or physical therapy aide, you need
- physical fitness
- good interpersonal skills
- manual dexterity
- empathy
- motivational skills
- ability to work hands-on with people

Do You Have What It Takes?

To be a physical therapist assistant or aide, you need to be physically fit enough to lift patients and to stand, kneel, or bend while working with patients throughout the day. You also need strong interpersonal skills so you can listen carefully to what patients are saying and help them understand how their prescribed therapies will help them get better.

A Typical Day at Work

To meet the needs of patients, physical therapy offices and clinics often are open early in the morning, at night, and on weekends. Consequently, physical therapist assistants and aides may need to work irregular hours. Most work in shifts, and work with a patient every half hour or so.

Depending on a patient's needs, a physical therapist assistant may help the patient do strengthening exercises or show him or her how to walk with a cane. A physical therapist aide will offer assistance as needed. He or she may, for example, help move a patient to a treatment area, confirm the next day's appointments, or place an order for new supplies.

How to Break In

While in high school, you can get a jump on your studies by taking biology, health, and science classes. Working in fitness centers or volunteering at rehab centers can also give you a feel for this field.

Enrolling in a two-year program that provides clinical training will help you gain the knowledge and on-the-job experience needed to work as a physical therapist assistant. While you're in school, you can become a student member of the American Physical Therapy Association. Doing so will give you a chance to learn more about your chosen field, meet other PTAs, and it might even lead to a job after graduation. The association even has a members-only Web section that offers career advice.

Two-Year Training

About 240 technical schools, community colleges, and trade schools offer accredited physical therapy programs leading to an associate's degree. While in school, you'll be required to take academic courses, such as algebra, anatomy, physiology, biology, chemistry, and psychology. You'll also work in clinical rotations, where you'll receive hands-on training that will teach you how to care for patients.

PTA licensing requirements vary from states to state. Depending on your state's regulations, you will need to complete a specific amount of educational and clinical training, be certified in CPR and first-aid, and pass specified exams.

Physical assistants usually receive their training while working, but as in any career, those who take related course-work in college, will have a competitive edge in the job market.

What to Look For in a School

When considering a two-year school, be sure to ask these questions:

☞ Does the school offer related coursework in subjects that will teach you how to work with and treat physical therapy patients?

☞ Is the school accredited by the Commission on Accreditation in Physical Therapy Education (CAPTE)?

☞ What is the school's job placement rate?

☞ Does the school provide clinical instruction? Is the equipment up-to-date?

☞ What are the instructors' credentials? Have they worked in the industry?

The Future

As the population ages—and people's bodies wear down—the demand for physical therapist assistants and aides is expected to grow. The growing push to keep medical costs down will boost job opportunities for physical therapist assistants who will be asked to take on many of the duties performed by higher-paid physical therapists. Physical therapist aides will also be needed with the best jobs going to those with the most experience and training.

"I always ask my patients: 'What is it that you want to be able to do?' If you think about it, that's why we're here. We're here to make them better."
—Carol Ann Everett, physical therapist assistant

Did You Know?

World War II and a nationwide polio epidemic created a huge demand for physical therapists in the 1940s and 1950s. During that period, membership in the nation's physical therapy organization rocketed from just under 1,000 in the late 1930s to 8,000. Today, more than 75,000 people are members of what is now known as the American Physical Therapy Association.

Interview with a Professional:
Q&A

Carol Ann Everett
Physical therapist assistant, Chicago, Illinois

Q: *How did you get started?*

A: I was an area director for Bally Total Fitness. I did personal training on the side. I realized that more and more people were coming in with injuries. So I started thinking about going into physical therapy. Then I had knee surgery and was in the hospital. A physical therapist tried to get me up. I tried to tell him I was really sick. He forced me to stand up and I threw up on him and he left.

When I left the hospital, the doctor said, "Here are some crutches." Nobody ever told me if I should do exercises or how I should do the stairs [leading to my apartment]. I figured out everything on my own. That's when I decided to go to a PTA school.

I paid my way through school. I worked in the morning at a health club and took classes at night.

Q: *What's a typical day like?*

A: I work four 10-hour days in an outpatient clinic. I start at 7 a.m. I stop at 5:30. I have a patient every half hour. Typically in the morning, I have my patients who are going to work. In mid-mornings, I generally have the orthopedics, the joint replacements, the hip replacements. In the afternoons, I get my athletes.

We have so much fun. I make up games for my patients. I make them do lunges to Abba's "Dancing Queen." We play stool crickets: I have my patients scoot on chairs. I take my patients outside. I'll have them run up the hill. I have found you have to be very creative to be a therapist.

I also work in management. I have to make sure all the other therapists are doing their work and handle customer service. My day goes back and forth between patient care and management.

I'm extremely busy but that's how I like it. I also teach part time. I teach professional communications for first-year PTA students. I try to teach them how to talk and write professionally.

Q: *What's your advice for those starting a career?*

A: The PTA is a two-year program. It's very accelerated and it's very intense. I always tell people who are going into physical therapy, that you need to commit to this. You can't skip class. You can't skip homework. You have to constantly keep up. You have a test or a practical most every class.

You really have to study. You really have to make the time commitment. The students who don't succeed are the ones who don't keep up with their work and don't ask for help. The people who try and ask for help, they get through it. On clinical rotations, your hours will be whatever your instructors' are. My students do four 10-hour days with me.

Have fun. Really listen to your patients. Figure out what they want to do. And have fun in therapy. Make them do silly things. Sometimes we make them do the hula hoop.

You've got to make it fun. Therapy is hard work. It's painful. It's a big chunk of your life, coming to therapy a half hour three times a week.

Q: What's the best part about being a physical therapist assistant?

A: I love my patients. My all-time favorite patient is this lady who had had both shoulders replaced. She wanted to bake cookies. She was like 90, and this poor woman could not lift her arms. So on one of her last therapy days, she came in with a bunch of cookies. I was crying because that's what she really wanted to do: Bake cookies. I had another lady who had both knees replaced and she wanted to stand up in restaurants. The patient said, "You don't know how embarrassing it is to have to have people pull you up in a restaurant."

Job Seeking Tips

See the suggestions below and turn to Appendix A for tips on creating a résumé, interviewing for schools or jobs, and collecting references.

✔ Decide what you're interested in and seek relevant experience.

✔ Seek advice from the career placement office.

✔ Become an active student member of professional organizations in your field.

✔ Check out the American Physical Therapy Association's online career center (http://www.apta.org)

Career Connections

For further information, contact the following organizations.

American Academy of Physical Therapy
http://www.aaptnet.org/home

American Physical Therapy Association http://www.apta.org

National Society of Allied Health (NSAH) http://www.nsah.org

Associate's Degree Programs

Here are a few schools offering quality physical therapy programs:

University of Pittsburgh at Titusville, Titusville, Pennsylvania

Gwinnett Technical College, Lawrenceville, Georgia

Spokane Falls Community College, Spokane, Washington

Jefferson State Community College, Birmingham, Alabama

Arapahoe Community College, Littleton, Colorado

Financial Aid

For more information on financial aid for two-year students, turn to Appendix B.

The **American Academy of Physical Therapy** awards scholarships to students enrolled in an approved entry-level PT or associate's degree PTA program with an interest in helping minority patients. http://www.aaptnet.org

The **American Physical Therapy Association** has a Minority Scholarship Fund, which helps minority students who are studying to become physical therapist assistants, and also offers the **Mary McMillan Scholarship Award** to APTA student members enrolled in physical therapy programs.   http://www.apta.org

Related Careers

Physical therapist, occupational therapist, occupational therapist assistant, pharmacy aide, pharmacy technician, and social service assistant.

Licensed Practical Nurse

Vital Statistics

Salary: The median salary for licensed practical nurses (LPNs) is about $34,000 a year, according to 2006 data from the U.S. Bureau of Labor Statistics.

Employment: The demand for licensed practical nurses is high and is expected to continue to grow.

Education: Accredited schools provide essential instruction and clinical training for people who want to work as licensed practical nurses. After graduation, you can become an LPN by passing a national written exam called the NCLEX-PN.

Work Environment: Nurses care for patients in hospitals, health clinics, doctor's offices, and other medical facilities. They often work long days and spend much of the day on their feet.

When you go to the doctor, a nurse is often the first person you see. He or she is the one who asks about your symptoms and takes your temperature and blood pressure. Depending on what the doctor orders, the nurse may also bandage a wound, give you a shot, or administer intravenous fluids.

Many of these tasks are performed by licensed practical nurses, or LPNs, who work under the supervision of doctors and registered nurses (RNs). LPNs work in hospitals, nursing homes, health care centers, doctor's offices, and other medical facilities where they help care for ill patients and people with disabilities.

LPNs do their best to make patients feel better. They feed and bathe patients who aren't able to do it themselves. They treat bedsores and give alcohol rubs and massages to bedridden patients. They help keep track of a patient's vital signs and monitor their reactions to medications and treatments. In doctors' offices, some LPNs also help answer phones, schedule appointments, and track patient records.

Gaining the skills needed to work as an LPN requires a mix of classroom instruction and clinical training at one of the 1,200 state-approved programs at colleges, technical schools, and other educational facilities throughout the United States. At some schools, you can complete your training in as little as one year. Other schools offer programs that lead to a two-year associate's degree. As part of your education, you'll receive clinical training in a hospital or other medical office. Under the supervision of a skilled nurse or doctor, you'll have a chance to care for patients with a variety of needs. Before you can be licensed to work as an LPN, you'll also need to pass a national exam, given by the National Council of State Boards of Nursing (NCSBN).

Of the 726,000 licensed practical nurses who work in the United States, the top wage earners make more than $46,000 a year. About 27 percent work in hospitals, 25 percent work in nursing care facilities, and 12 percent work in doctor's offices. Some also work for home health care services, employment services, and community care facilities for the elderly.

No matter where LPNs work, their days are often long, difficult, and stressful. In spite of the pressures, the best nurses love their jobs because they get great satisfaction from helping others in need.

"Nurses are patient people."
—Author unknown

On the Job

Licensed practical nurses look after the physical and emotional needs of their patients. They observe, record, and share information about a patient's symptoms with the patient's doctor or registered nurse. They take and record a patient's temperature, blood pressure, pulse, and respiration rate. They also may dress a patient's wounds, give the patient medicine, update a patient's chart, and assemble and use catheters, tracheotomy tubes, oxygen machines, and other medical equipment.

In a hospital, LPNs record a patient's food and fluid intake, apply compresses, bathe and dress patients, and collect laboratory specimens. They also help patients walk and do basic range of motion exercises.

In doctors' offices, some LPNs make appointments and keep medical records, while in nursing homes, they often assess residents' needs and supervise the care provided by nursing aides.

Keys to Success

To be a successful licensed practical nurse, you need
- physical strength
- stamina
- compassion
- self-confidence
- good judgment
- decision-making skills
- ability to work hands-on with people

Do You Have What It Takes?

To be an LPN, you need to be a caring, compassionate person who will look out for the needs of your patients. You need to know how to communicate with the patients, their families, and the other medical workers. You need to be emotionally strong enough to handle the stress that comes from working with the sick and injured.

A Typical Day at Work

Nurses work in hospitals, doctor's offices, health clinics, schools, and wherever else patients need care. Because patients may require medical care at any time of the day or night, some nurses work nights, weekends, and holidays and may put in 12-hour days.

How to Break In

While in high school, you can start preparing for a career in nursing by taking courses in science and math. You also can gain valuable experience by volunteering or working part time in a nursing home, a clinic, or other medical facility.

Once you start college, become an active student member of professional associations, such as the National Association for Practical Nurse Education and Service (NAPNES) and the National Student Nurses' Association (NSNA). Doing so will give you a chance to meet others in your field and often can lead to professional contacts, who may be able to help you land a job.

Two-Year Training

Classroom instruction coupled with clinical training can prepare you for a career as a licensed practical nurse. While in school, you'll study basic nursing concepts. You'll learn how to administer drugs, provide first aid, and give nutritional advice. You'll also learn about anatomy, physiology, medical-surgical nursing, pediatrics, and obstetrics. During your clinical training, you'll have a chance to care for patients under the supervision of registered nurses and doctors in a hospital or other medical facility.

Once you finish your training, you'll be eligible to take the NCLEX-PN licensing exam administered by the National Council of State Boards of Nursing (NCSBN).

If you think you may eventually want to pursue a four-year degree, make sure that the credits you earn in your two-year program can be applied to a four-year degree.

What to Look For in a School

When considering a two-year school, be sure to ask these questions:

☞ Does the school offer work-related courses and clinical training that prepare you to care for patients in a variety of settings?

☞ Is the program accredited or approved by your state's licensing board or the National League for Nursing Accrediting Commission?

☞ What is the school's job placement rate?

☞ Will the program prepare you to take and pass the required licensing examination in your field?

☞ What are the instructors' credentials? Have they worked in the industry? Have they kept up with new techniques and procedures in the industry? Are they available outside the classroom?

☞ Do the classrooms and labs have up-to-date equipment?

☞ If you think you may want to continue your schooling, can the credits be transferred to a bachelor's degree program?

The Future

As the population continues to age, the demand for LPNs in facilities that care for the elderly and patients with disabilities is expected to be especially strong. LPNs also will be needed to care for elderly people who continue to live at home.

Thanks to improved technology, doctor's offices and outpatient health centers are starting to perform more medical procedures outside hospitals, which will create a bigger demand for LPNs in these facilities.

Did You Know?

In 1860, Florence Nightingale wrote *Notes on Nursing,* which described the principles of nursing as being careful observation and sensitivity to the patient's needs. The book, which has been translated into eleven languages, is still in print today, available from the Florence Nightingale Museum in London.

Interview with a Professional:
Q&A

Adrian Cowen

Licensed practical nurse, Hudson Valley Hospital
Center, Cortlandt Manor, New York

Q: *How did you get started?*

A: I worked in a doctor's office for five years. I was basically the reception-ist/insurance biller. I would bring the patients in and get them set up for the doctor to come in. And one day, I decided, I could do this. I went back to school. I worked days and did night classes, which took about 10 months. And I got my practical nursing certificate or degree. I studied for the board, and here I am.

Q: *What's a typical day like?*

A: I work three days a week, 12-hours shifts. I get up about 5:30 in the morning, I get my daughter to the sitter and then I have to be at work at 7. I'm there until 7:15, 7:30 at night.

I try to learn as much as I can while taking care of my patients. I look at what the RNs are doing so I have an idea of what it entails so I know every-thing that goes on. I'm always available. I know just about everything that's going on with my patients. I'm a patient's advocate. I try to do as much as I can for my patients. I make sure my patients are comfortable within my 12-hour shift.

Q: *What's your advice for those starting a career?*

A: You really need to look within yourself and make sure this is something you want to do and something you can do. Nursing is taking care of people and everything that entails. I don't just give medical care. I will empty a bedpan. I will clean feces. It's not the prettiest job.

Look into yourself and make sure this is something you can do. It's not just standing there, looking pretty. You really have to get into it. You may have a patient go into crisis. You can't panic and go into shock. You have to be able to make decisions. You have to be a quick thinker and move be-cause someone's life is at stake.

Make sure when you're just starting a job to be on a medical surgical floor. I cherish every day I'm on a medical surgical unit. It's the hardest unit in the hospital, but you get a little bit of everything. There's the cancer pa-tient; there's the diabetes patient; there's the fractured hip. If you can han-dle a medical surgical unit, you will be able to handle any unit in a hospital or any nursing home.

Q: What's the best part about being an LPN?

A: You change lives. People are very grateful that you helped them in the smallest way. They're grateful, and in the end, that makes you feel good. You know you've made a difference.

Job Seeking Tips

See the suggestions below and turn to Appendix A for tips on creating a résumé, interviewing for schools or jobs, and collecting references.

✔ Decide what you're interested in and seek relevant experience.

✔ Seek advice from the career placement office.

✔ Reach out to associations in your chosen field.

✔ Take the steps required to become licensed in your field,

Career Connections

For further information, contact the following organizations.

MinorityNurse.com http://www.minoritynurse.com

National Association for Practical Nurse Education and Service, Inc. http://www.napnes.org

National Council of State Boards of Nursing http://www.ncsbn.org

National Federation of Licensed Practical Nurses, Inc. http://www.nflpn.org

National League for Nursing http://www.nln.org

National League for Nursing Accrediting Commission http://www.nlnac.org

National Student Nurses' Association http://www.nsna.org

Associate's Degree Programs

Here are a few schools offering quality nursing programs.

Greenville Technical College, Greenville, South Carolina

Albuquerque Technical Vocational Institute, Albuquerque, New Mexico

Pennsylvania College of Technology, Williamsport, Pennsylvania

Cincinnati State Technical & Community College, Cincinnati, Ohio

Financial Aid

Here are a few nursing scholarships. For more on financial aid, turn to Appendix B.

The federal government's **Nursing Scholarship Program** pays tuition and other educational costs to nursing students who agree to work at least two years in a health facility with a critical shortage of nurses. http://bhpr.hrsa.gov/nursing/scholarship/

The **Foundation of the National Student Nurses' Association** awards a Frances Tompkins Memorial Scholarship to students pursuing a degree in nursing.   http://www.nsna.org/foundation

Related Careers

Emergency medical technician, paramedic, medical assistant, nursing aide, health aide, registered nurse, licensed vocational nurse, social and human service assistant, and surgical technician.

Surgical Technologist

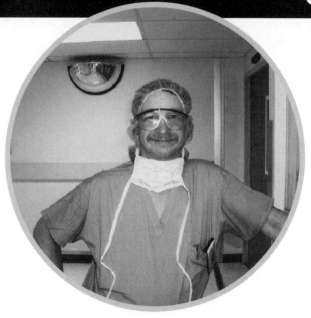

Vital Statistics

Salary: The median salary for a surgical technologist is about $34,000 a year, according to 2006 data from the U.S. Bureau of Labor Statistics.

Employment: The need for skilled surgical technologists will be excellent, with the demand growing faster than the average pace for other jobs through 2014.

Education: Accredited schools provide essential instruction and training for those who want to pursue a career in surgical technology.

Work Environment: A surgical technologist works in clean, well-lit rooms in hospitals, health clinics, and outpatient care centers. They often spend much of the day standing over patients during surgery.

If you've ever watched *Grey's Anatomy* or *ER,* you've seen a surgical technician working alongside surgeons and nurses in the operating room. Also commonly referred to as surgical technicians, surgical assistants or scrubs, a surgical technologist hands the surgeon needed instruments and supplies during an operation. Depending on the tech's level of expertise, the surgeon may ask the technician to help cut a tissue, close a wound, or insert a drainage tube.

You can acquire the skills needed to work as a surgical assistant at a community college, trade school, or technical school. Some programs can be finished in about 10 months, while programs that lead to an associate's degree take about two years. No matter which route you go, be sure to choose an accredited school that's affiliated with health organizations in your area. The Commission on Accreditation of Allied Health Education Programs (CAAHEP) has approved more than 400 such schools, providing you with numerous options. In school, you'll take courses that will prepare you to work in an operating room. You'll study physiology, professional ethics, medical terminology, and similar subjects in class. You'll do clinical rotations, where you'll learn how to sterilize instruments, work with surgical equipment, and prepare patients for surgery.

After completing an accredited program, you'll be eligible to take a national certification exam given by the National Board of Surgical Technology and Surgical Assisting. Passing this exam qualifies you as a certified surgical technologist (CST). You also can take an exam, administered by the National Center for Competency Testing, to qualify as a tech in surgery-certified (TS-C).

About 84,000 surgical technologists work in the United States, with the majority working in operating and delivery rooms in hospitals. Others assist doctors and dentists who perform outpatient surgery. The best-paid surgical techs make more than $46,000 a year.

An elite few, commonly referred to as "private scrubs," work directly for surgeons on surgical teams who perform specialized procedures, such as liver transplants and plastic surgery. Some techs are even recruited to work as temporary travel scrubs, who are paid premium wages to fill in at short-staffed hospitals across the country.

On the Job

As a surgical technologist, you'll prepare the operating room before surgery. You'll lay out the surgical equipment, put X-rays in place, and make sure the surgical equipment is working. You'll also help patients get ready for surgery by washing, shaving, and disinfecting their incision sites; moving them to the operating rooms; and placing them on operating tables.

During surgery, technologists pass instruments and other sterile supplies to surgeons. They count the number of sponges, needles, supplies, and instruments in the operating room, and help prepare specimens for laboratory analysis. Surgical technologists sometimes help close wounds, insert drainage tubes, clamp tissues, and even help resuscitate patients in cardiac arrest. After an operation, surgical technologists transfer the patient to the recovery room, and clean and restock the operating room.

Keys to Success

To be a successful surgical technician, you need
- manual dexterity
- emotional stability
- conscientiousness
- ability to work under pressure
- physical fitness
- critical thinking ability
- stamina
- good communication skills
- medical knowledge

Do You Have What It Takes?

If you're the type of person who faints at the sight of blood or when dissecting a frog, then this profession may not be for you. To work as a surgical technician, you also need to be a fast, careful worker who can handle life-

and-death situations. Good eye-hand coordination and fine motor skills are essential to deftly handle the instruments used during surgery. You also must be able to read people and situations well, so you know which instrument a surgeon needs without being told.

A Typical Day at Work

Surgical technologists work in clean, well-lit operating and delivery rooms in hospitals. Some also work in outpatient care centers and emergency rooms. During surgery, they often must stand for long periods of time and must stay alert throughout the entire operation. Sometimes the technician's 40-hour workweek stretches into nights, weekends, and holidays.

How to Break In

You can get a jump on your career while still in high school by taking courses in health, biology, chemistry, and mathematics. Any experience at a medical facility—even volunteering—will come in handy. Even though you may not be able to work in a surgical department, being around other medical professionals will give you a better understanding of the medical field.

Once you've started work on your degree, you can become a student member of the Association of Surgical Technologists (http://www.ast.org). Becoming an active member will give you access to career advice, job boards, and other professionals in the field. In fact, you may very well end up meeting someone who can help you find your first job.

When you finish your education, make the extra effort to become certified in your field. Being able to say you're a certified surgical technologist (CST) or tech in surgery-certified (TS-C) lets prospective employers know you've acquired the skills needed to do the job. With advanced training and experience, surgical techs can also become certified as first assistants, who are trained to help treat and close wounds, suture cuts, cauterize bleeders, and perform other surgical duties.

Two-Year Training

Enrolling in an accredited program at a community college or vocational school can prepare you to work as a surgical technologist. The trick is to make sure you enroll in one of the more than 400 programs that have been accredited by the Commission on Accreditation of Allied Health Education Programs (CAAHEP). The programs vary in length: Some programs provide a certificate in just nine months, while other more extensive programs offer an associate's degree in two years.

Be careful when choosing a program. Some so-called "diploma mills" and "accreditation mills" make misleading promises. Legitimate schools, however, will provide you with the training you'll need to work in this field. While in school, you'll take courses in subjects, such as microbiology and medical terminology, and also receive hands-on clinical training. You'll study subjects such as anatomy, physiology, pharmacology, and professional ethics. During your clinical training, you'll learn how to sterilize instruments, prevent infections, and work with different drugs and equipment.

After completing an accredited program, you'll be eligible to take a national certification exam given by the National Board of Surgical Technology and Surgical Assisting (NBSTSA). Passing this exam earns you the Certified Surgical Technologist (CST) certification. Because the medical profession is constantly changing, CSTs must be recertified every four years. Advanced certification as a tech in surgery-certified (TS-C) is also available through a national exam administered by National Center for Competency Testing. This certification must be renewed every five years.

"I don't dawdle. I'm a surgeon. I make an incision, do what needs to be done, and sew up the wound. There is a beginning, a middle and an end."
—Richard Selzer, surgeon and author of several books, including *Confessions of a Knife.*

What to Look For in a School

When considering a two-year school, be sure to ask these questions:

☞ Does the school offer related course-work in subjects that will prepare you to assist surgeons?

☞ What is the school's job placement rate?

☞ What are the instructors' credentials? Have they worked in the industry?

☞ Has the school's program been accredited by CAAHEP?

☞ Is the school affiliated with an allied health organization, such as the American College of Surgeons, the American Medical Association, or the American College of Physicians?

☞ Does the school prepare students to earn certification in their field or specialty?

Interview with a Professional:
Q&A

Richard Hutson

Certified surgical technologist, St. Anthony Central
Hospital, Denver, Colorado

Q: *How did you get started?*

A: I was watching TV one night and I saw a commercial for the surgical technician program at Concorde College. I said, "I can do that." I called Concorde and scheduled an interview. It was great timing. Their next class was starting like within a week, and they had an opening, and I took it. I can't believe I could have been doing this job all my life. I totally love this job.

Q: *What's a typical day like?*

A: I go in the afternoons. What I'll do usually is I'll finish up some of the scheduled cases, and then I'll do the unscheduled cases: the traumas, whatever's coming into the ER that has to do with surgery. We do a lot of automobile accidents. We get the gunshots, the stabbings, everything you can imagine.

I'm the scrub tech, so I set all the instruments up. I make sure everything is sterile and assist the surgeon during surgery. Sometimes they'll have a surgical assistant. Sometimes they won't, depending on the complexity of the case. I kind of act as an assistant and as a scrub tech at the same time.

We're right there right on top of the patient, standing next to the physician. And if he says, "Reach in and hold the liver out of the way," I reach in and hold the liver out of the way. When we get done, I help them patch up the patient. We send him off and do the next one.

Some nights, it's just constant. It's never-ending. And some nights, it's just not. You never know. A month ago, we had 15 motorcycle accidents in just seven days at our hospital.

Q: *What's your advice for those starting a career?*

A: Try to go and observe a surgery before you do it. Because you don't know if you may one of those people who passes out cold from seeing a lot of blood or seeing somebody cut open. I think students should know that before you spend $20,000 going to school. If you're going to hit the floor, it's no good. It's like being a pilot with degenerative eye disease.

You have to decide what you want: Whether you want the rush like the stuff they show on *ER* on TV or whether you want to make a lot of money. If you're willing to travel, or work in certain areas, you can make over $100,000 within two or three years.

Q: *What's the best part about being a surgical technician?*

A: It's a massive rush when somebody comes in and they're "dead," and five minutes later, they're alive because of something you participated in. I reached the top of my career ladder in about two years because I don't want ever want to do anything else.

The Future

Advances in fiber optics and laser technology will encourage the development of new surgical procedures, which will in turn lead to a demand for surgical assistants. Plus, as the baby-boom population ages, their need for surgery will grow, which will also create a demand for more surgical assistants.

Did You Know?

According to Guinness World Records, the longest medical operation lasted more than 96 hours. During the operation in Chicago, Illinois, surgeons removed an ovarian cyst from a patient. The operation started on February 4, 1951, and ended on February 8. Thanks to the cyst's removal, the patient's weight dropped from 616 pounds to 308 pounds!

Job Seeking Tips

See the suggestions below and turn to Appendix A for advice on résumés, and interviews.

✔ Decide what you're interested in and seek relevant experience.

✔ Seek advice from the career placement office.

✔ Become an active student member of professional associations, such as the Association of Surgical Technologists.

Career Connections

For further information, contact the following organizations.

Accreditation Review Committee on Education in Surgical Technology http://www.arcst.org

Association of Surgical Technologists http://www.ast.org

The National Board of Surgical Technology and Surgical Assisting (NBSTSA) http://www.lcc-st.org

Associate's Degree Programs

Here are a few schools offering quality surgical technology programs:

Virginia College-Birmingham, Birmingham, Alabama

Lamson College, Tempe, Arizona

Ivy Tech Community College-Kokomo, Kokomo, Indiana

Flathead Valley Community College, Kalispell, Montana

Montgomery County Community College, Pottstown, Pennsylvania

Laramie County Community College, Cheyenne, Wyoming

Financial Aid

Here are a few surgical technology scholarships. For more on financial aid, turn to Appendix B.

The **Association of Surgical Technologists (AST) National Honor Society Scholarship** goes to AST Honor Society members enrolled in a surgical assisting program. http://www.ast.org/Content/Education/Scholarships.htm

The **Foundation for Surgical Technology** awards scholarships to students in CAAHEP-accredited surgical technology programs. http://www.ast.org/Content/Education/Scholarships.htm

Thompson Delmar Learning Surgical Technology Student Scholarship goes to students enrolled in accredited surgical technology programs. http://www.ast.org/Content/Education/Scholarships.htm

Related Careers

Dental assistant, licensed practical nurse, licensed vocational nurse, clinical laboratory technologist, and medical assistant.

Dialysis Technician

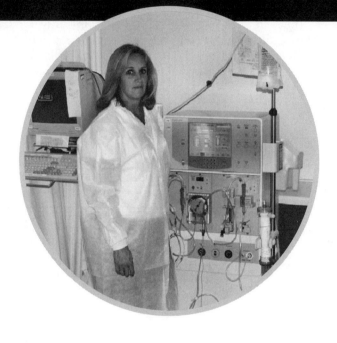

Vital Statistics

Salary: The median salary for dialysis technicians is about $29,000 a year, according to 2006 data from Salary.com.

Employment: The job outlook for certified dialysis technicians is good and expected to continue to grow.

Education: State-approved programs at community colleges, technical schools, and medical facilities provide training for people who want to work as dialysis technicians. Students can often complete their training in two semesters.

Work Environment: Dialysis technicians work in hospitals, clinics, and other medical facilities that offer dialysis treatment; some also travel to patients' homes. Because dialysis technicians work with blood, they must follow strict safety guidelines to avoid contracting or spreading hepatitis, AIDS, and other infectious diseases.

Your kidneys work around the clock to keep your body clean. They filter out extra water, minerals, and toxins that are dumped into the blood each day. During the course of a day, your hard-working kidneys will process 18 gallons of blood an hour, and produce as much as seven gallons of urine.

However, diseases such as high blood pressure and diabetes sometimes weaken the kidneys so that they can no longer do their job. When that happens, patients often require dialysis, a mechanical process that does the work of a kidney. The person who performs these dialysis treatments is called a dialysis technician.

The most popular form of dialysis is called *hemodialysis*. During this procedure, a patient's blood is drained into a special machine with two sections. The blood goes into one side of the machine; the particles of waste in the blood go into the other side, which contains a fluid called *dialysate*. A thin membrane separates the two sides. As the blood goes through the machine, the waste in the blood goes through the microscopic holes in the membrane and is washed away in the dialysate. The blood cells, which are too big to go through the membrane, are sent back to the body.

The length of treatment varies depending on the patient's needs. Patients whose kidneys are temporarily damaged may receive dialysis until their kidneys have had a chance to recover, while those with chronic renal diseases receive dialysis on an ongoing basis. The only other long-term alternative is a kidney transplant, which isn't always an option, because of a patient's poor health or a shortage of available kidneys.

As a dialysis technician, you work the machines that remove the waste and excess fluids from the blood of patients whose kidneys can no longer do so. You must have a thorough understanding of the dialysis equipment, or *dialyzer*, which functions as a patient's artificial kidney. You are responsible for keeping the machines in good working order, and cleaning and sterilizing them after each use. You also look after your patients' well-being, monitoring and recording their vital signs before, during, and after the blood-cleansing process.

Some dialysis workers specialize as patient care technicians (PCTs), who care for patients undergoing dialysis. Working under the supervision of a registered nurse, they help prepare a patient for dialysis and monitor them during the treatment. To be a PCT, you must understand the science behind dialysis treatment as well as the dialysis process, and be able to respond to a patient's physical and emotional needs during treatment.

To become certified to work in this field, you must take approved medical courses and pass exams give by the Board of Nephrology Examiners-Nursing-Technology (BONENT), the National Nephrology Certification Organization (NNCO), and/or the Nephrology Nursing Certification Commission (NNCC). While certification is voluntary, taking the time to gain certification helps establish you as a skilled professional. Initial training for basic care can often be completed in two semesters. Students who pursue additional education and training, however, have a competitive advantage.

> **"You're either going to love this career or hate it. There's no happy medium. It's a tough job because you're taking care of sick patients. You see those same sick patients every single week, three times a week for years. It's very hard to watch someone you've taken care of for years diminish."**
> —Cynthia Hoplock, C.H.T., bio-medical technician

On the Job

As a dialysis technician, your job is to make sure the machines and supplies needed for dialysis treatments are in good working order. You must clean, sterilize, and inspect the equipment before and after each use. You help the patient care technicians set up each machine and connect it to a patient. Working with prescriptions and unit rules, you calculate and adjust the fluid remove rates, measure and adjust blood flow rates, and administer anticoagulants to keep the blood from clotting. During dialysis, you monitor a patient's vital signs and blood flow, making sure everything is going as planned. If a problem arises, you seek advice from the supervising registered nurse or doctor. Once the patient's dialysis is complete, you disconnect the patient, discard the used supplies, and sanitize the equipment, so it'll be ready for the next patient.

 Keys to Success

To be a successful dialysis technician, you need
- physical fitness
- emotionally stability
- an empathetic nature
- ability to work under stress
- attention to detail and safety

A Typical Day at Work

During a typical shift as a dialysis technician, you prepare the dialysis machines for incoming patients. You check the equipment to make sure it's clean and in working order. You test the alarms, the conductivity, and the temperature settings on the monitors and machines.

When a patient arrives, you check pre-dialysis vital signs, weight, and temperature. You administer local anesthesia, insert the needles, and start the patient's dialysis treatment. During the patient's treatment, you measure and adjust the blood flow rates, calculate and adjust the fluid removal rates, and monitor the patient's vial signs. You also keep an eye out for emergencies, such as a blood leak or a blood clot.

When the patient's dialysis treatment is done, you check the patient's vital signs, temperature, and weight, and let the supervising nurse know about any emotional, nutritional, or medical concerns that the patient may have mentioned during the treatment. Then the equipment must be returned to the reuse room, where you clean and sterilize it, so it's ready for the next patient.

In some medical centers, the workers specialize. Reuse specialists set up and clean the machines while patient treatment care workers focus on monitoring the patients during their treatment.

Do You Have What It Takes?

To work as a dialysis technician, you must be in good enough shape to stand for long periods of time and lift heavy objects. You gave to be a careful worker who can be counted on to accurately track vital signs, administer prescribed treatments, and thoroughly clean and sterilize the dialysis equipment. Working with patients who are very ill requires that you walk an emotional tightrope: You need to provide an empathetic ear while still maintaining a professional relationship. You also must have an appreciation for helping people overcome illness.

How to Break In

You can start getting ready for a career as a dialysis technician while still in high school. Taking courses in math, biology, and communications, for example, will give you skills that will come in handy in your profession. You also can seek a part-time job or do volunteer work at health care clinics, hospitals, and other medical facilities.

Professional organizations in your field can provide you with helpful information on educational programs, scholarships, and jobs. Good bets include the National Kidney Foundation, the Board of Nephrology Examiners Nursing and Technology (BONENT), and the National Nephrology Certification Organization. These organizations also offer courses, seminars, and other educational opportunities that can help you develop your skills, leading to jobs with more responsibility and higher wages.

Two-Year Training

Community colleges, technical schools, and in-house training programs at medical facilities can often train you to become a certified dialysis worker in just two semesters. Many of these schools offer continued study and training, which can lead to advanced certification and associate's degree programs in related health fields.

Students enrolled in a dialysis technician program take courses that teach them how to care for patients who need dialysis. During training, you'll explore both the theory (the reasons why) and the practical (how to do the work) of a dialysis technician. You'll learn how to select and operate the dialysis equipment and how to monitor a patient's vital signs. You'll also learn the basics of respiratory and circulatory physiology.

To establish yourself as a trained professional, you'll need to earn certification from one (or more) professional organizations. The Nephrology Nursing Certification Commission (NNCC) offers a Certified Clinical Hemodialysis Technician (CCHT) exam that you can take after six months of experience. The Board of Nephrology Examiners Nursing and Technology (BONENT) offers an exam that qualifies you as a certified hemodialysis technician (CHT) after 12 months of experience. And the National Nephrology Certification Organization (NNCO) gives exams for the Certified in Clinical Nephrology Technology (CCNT) and Certified in Biomedical Nephrology Technology (CBNT) designations.

What to Look For in a School

When considering a two-year school, be sure to ask these questions:

☞ Does the school offer related course-work that will teach you how to work the dialysis equipment and care for dialysis patients?

☞ Does the school have a partnership with a local dialysis facility, where you can develop and practice your skills under the watchful eye of a trained instructor?

☞ What is the school's job placement rate?

☞ What are the instructors' credentials? Have they worked in the industry?

☞ Does the school offer the tools needed for hands-on learning?

☞ Does the school provide an opportunity to take college courses that will lead to an associate's degree in the health field?

The Future

A push for stricter standards in equipment and certification requirements will provide more opportunities for dialysis technicians with solid training and advanced certifications. Also, as our elderly population grows and requires medical attention, a larger segment of Americans may need dialysis treatment.

Job Seeking Tips

See the suggestions below and turn to Appendix A for advice on résumés, and interviews.

✔ Seek advice from the career placement office.

✔ Reach out, and when possible, join, professional associations in your field.

✔ Decide what you're interested in and seek relevant experience.

✔ Seek certification from organizations in your field, such as the Board of Nephrology Examiners Nursing and Technology (http://www .bonent.org/), the Nephrology Nursing Certification Commission (http://www.nncc-exam.org), and the National Nephrology Certification Organization (http://www.ptcny.com/clients/NNCO/).

✔ Combine your educational training with a clinical work, so you receive hands-on experience.

Interview with a Professional:
Q&A
Cynthia Hoplock
Bio-medical technician, Renal Institute of Central Jersey, Toms River, New Jersey

Q: *How did you get started?*

A: About 10 years ago, I was an EMT. I had a friend who was an educator at a hospital. She knew my heart was in helping people so she asked me if I would be interested in becoming a technician.

I was a sponge, wanting to learn everything. Wherever there was a seminar, I would go.

Two years ago, I was promoted to bio-med technician. I've run the gamut. I went from reuse technician to patient care to repairing machines. The only thing I haven't done yet is manage the facility.

Q: *What's a typical day like?*

A: In the reuse department, you're going in at 4 in the morning, to set up eight of the 32 machines. You're getting them ready for the patients to go on, making sure the water is ready to use. You put the patients on. You have four patients to put on in the morning. Once they're on, we monitor those four patients until the patient care technician comes in. Then we go back in and start re-processing any dialyzers that are low on content.

We get the machines ready and back in reuse by 7. By 8:30 or 9, we have dialyzers that are ready to come off. As the patient comes off, we go and collect the dirty dialyzers. We bring them back to the reuse room and rinse them free of blood. We clean them and test them to make sure they're ready for the next treatments.

If you're working the floor as a patient care technician, you go in and prep eight machines. You have four patient mods, which means you're responsible for four patients. You put those patients on, take those patients off. In the course of the day, you would have 12 patients. We work three 13-hours days. You work long days. You're on your feet all day. If you don't love what you're doing, there's no sense doing it.

Q: *What's your advice for those starting a career?*

A: The first thing is to get certified. When you have that certificate, it says you know what you're doing. You've gone through the courses. You've kept taking courses to keep up with your certification. When a patient comes in and knows that you know what you're doing, it calms him down to know that you're a professional.

(continued on next page)

(continued from previous page)

Q: *What's the best part about being a dialysis technician?*

A: For me, there's versatility. I don't come in and do one thing all day long. I need to be challenged and there are a lot of challenges in dialysis. I love the patients. I love talking with them. I love to be able to fix things. If something has gone wrong, there's a challenge to figure it out so that the rest of the day goes fine. That's what I love about it; there's always something going on.

Did You Know?

A Dutch physician, Willem J. Kolff, developed the first successful artificial kidney in the 1940s during World War II. Because his country was occupied by Nazi Germany, he had to improvise. For example, he used sausage casing to create the semi-permeable membrane that let the bad particles out while keeping the blood in.

Career Connections

For further information, contact the following organizations.

American Nephrology Nurses' Association http://www.annanurse.org

Board of Nephrology Examiners, Inc. Nursing and Technology http://www.bonent.org

National Association of Nephrology Technicians/Technologists http://www.dialysistech.org

National Kidney Foundation http://www.kidney.org

Nephrology Nursing Certification Commission (NNCC) http://www.nncc-exam.org

Nephrology News and Issues http://www.nephnews.com

Associate's Degree Programs

Here are a few quality programs in dialysis technology. (Most schools offer dialysis technology courses that lead to a certificate or diploma in the specialty, along with two-year degrees in the health field.)

Clover Park Technical College, Lakewood, Washington

Malcom X College, Chicago, Illinois

Niagara County Community College, Sanborn, New York

Sinclair Community College, Dayton, Ohio

Wilson Technical Community College, Wilson, North Carolina

Financial Aid

For more on financial aid for two-year students, turn to Appendix B.

The **Board of Nephrology Examiners Nursing and Technology (BO-NENT)** awards the Wesley Watkins Scholarship to members who write winning essays on an assigned topic.   http://www.bonent.org/about_"us/scholarship.html

Related Careers

Cardiovascular technologist, clinical laboratory technician, medical assistant, and licensed practical nurse.

Medical Records/ Health Information Technician

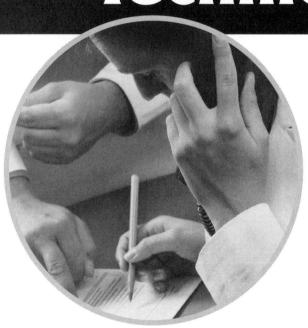

Vital Statistics

Salary: The median annual salary for medical records/health information technicians is about $25,600, according to 2006 data from the U.S. Bureau of Labor Statistics.

Employment: The demand for medical records/health information technicians is high and is expected to continue to grow. Workers who are skilled in medical coding will be especially sought after.

Education: Accredited schools provide essential instruction and training for people who want to work as medical records/health information technicians.

Work Environment: Medical records/health information technicians work in offices in hospitals, health clinics, doctor's offices, and other medical facilities.

Medical records technicians play a vital, behind-the-scenes role in a patient's medical care. They make sure a patient's medical records are filled out completely and filed properly. When a doctor or insurance company needs to review a record, they make the information available. They also safeguard patients' privacy, keeping medical records away from curiosity seekers who don't have permission to see the files.

A growing demand for increasingly sophisticated medical records from insurance companies, medical specialists, and patients has made the already crucial job of a medical records technician even more vital. In fact, top earners in the field make more than $41,700 a year.

As health care has become more high-tech and cost-conscious, some medical records technicians have started specializing in medical coding. Commonly referred to as health information coders, medical record coders or coding specialists, these technicians use computer software to assign a patient one of several hundred diagnosis-related groups, which in turn determines how much of the treatment is covered by insurance or Medicare. Because of the specialized nature and importance of this work, skilled coders are in great demand.

You can obtain the skills needed to work as a medical record specialist in an accredited two-year program at a community college, trade school, or technical school. In addition, some medical facilities provide on-the-job training to entry-level employees who show an aptitude for record-keeping.

During school, you'll take courses in communications, record-keeping, and medical terminology that will prepare you to handle a variety of medical records in hospitals, nursing homes, and doctor's offices. After completing your training, you'll be eligible to take a written exam offered by the American Health Information Management Association (AHIMA). Students who pass the exam earn the right to be called registered health information technicians (RHITs), which gives them an edge when seeking jobs and better wages.

Of the 159,000 medical records and health information technicians in the United States, about 40 percent work in hospitals. Many also work in doctor's offices, nursing care facilities, health care centers, and for home health care services. While a medical records technician's job isn't as glamorous or fast-paced as that of a paramedic or surgeon, the careful keeping and sharing of medical records plays an important role in safeguarding our health and privacy.

On the Job

Medical records technicians make sure patients' medical records are complete, accurate, and properly filed. They make sure a patient's medical charts have the required information, and that they are properly identified and have the necessary signatures. They also field requests made via phone, fax, e-mail, and in person from doctors, insurance workers, and patients seeking medical information.

Some technicians specialize in medical codes needed for insurance. They use their knowledge of diseases, insurance, and approved medical practices to assign codes to different diagnoses and treatments. They work with computer software to assign patients a diagnosis-related group (DRG), which determines how much a patient's insurance will pay for a specific treatment.

Other tech-savvy medical record workers use computer software to analyze data, which can help medical caregivers improve patient care, control costs, respond to surveys, or do research.

The exact role of a technician depends on where he or she works. In a small practice, a technician may handle most of the information, while in a larger clinic or hospital, he or she might specialize in one area or supervise health information clerks and transcriptionists.

Medi-Smart, an online source for nurses (http://medi-smart.com/med record.htm), lists funny physicians' quotes taken from actual medical records. A sampling:

- The patient refused an autopsy.
- She is numb from her toes down.
- The skin was moist and dry.
- On the second day the knee was better and on the third day it completely disappeared.

Keys to Success

To be a successful medical records technician, you need

- organizational ability
- communication skills
- multitasking talents
- attention to detail
- high regard for confidentiality

Do You Have What It Takes?

To work in the medical records field, you need to be a detail-oriented person who can quickly and accurately organize information in a usable form. You also need to be able to effectively communicate with other medical workers, insurance agents, and doctors. Most importantly, you need to be someone who can be trusted to maintain a patient's confidentiality.

A Typical Day at Work

As a medical records technician, you generally work 40-hour work weeks. In today's high-tech society, you spend much of your day in front of a computer. Your eyes may get a bit tired by the end of the day as you spend most of your time reviewing medical records—making sure they are all properly completed. A big part of your job is knowing all the medical coding for different procedures, ailments, etc. Although you spend most of your time with a computer, you're also popular with doctors, insurance workers, and patients who need the info you keep track of. They keep you busy sending a steady stream of faxes, e-mail, and in-person requests.

How to Break In

You can get a jump on your career plans while still in high school by taking job-related subjects, such as biology, writing, and computing. You also can try to find time to volunteer or work part time at a medical facility. Even if you do nothing more than answer phones or sell items in the hospital gift shop, you'll have a chance to work in a medical environment, and may very well meet contacts who can help you find a good job once your schooling is complete.

Becoming an active student member of the professional association in your field can also help you gain a foothold in your career. When you graduate from school, be sure to take the national exam for the Registered Health Information Technician (RHIT) credential, which is administered by the American Health Information Management Association (AHIMA). Gaining certification as an RHIT shows prospective employers that you have mastered the skills needed to do the job and take your profession seriously.

You can continue to build up your credentials and employment prospects by passing exams for other certifications, including Registered Health Administrator, Certified Coding Associate, and the Certified in HealthCare and Security credential.

Two-Year Training

As medical record keeping has become more sophisticated, so has the need for specialized training. Enrolling in a two-year program that focuses on medical information can help you get started on the right career path. During your studies, you'll take courses in communications, writing, record-keeping, computing, and medical terminology. You'll learn how to handle a variety of medical records in hospitals, doctor's offices, nursing homes, and other medical facilities.

After completing your training, you'll be eligible to take a written exam offered by American Health Information Management Association (AHIMA). Students who qualify as registered health information technicians (RHITs) will have an edge over noncertified workers when looking for jobs.

What to Look For in a School

When considering a two-year school, be sure to ask these questions:

☞ Does the school offer work-related courses that will help you learn how to handle medical records, including ones that are computerized?

☞ Is the school accredited by the Commission on Accreditation for Health Informatics and Information Management Education (CAHIIM)?

☞ What is the school's job placement rate?

☞ Will the program prepare you to take and pass the certification exams in your chosen field?

☞ What are the instructors' credentials? Have they worked in the industry? Have they kept up with new techniques and procedures in the industry? Are they available outside the classroom?

☞ Do the classrooms have up-to-date computer equipment?

Interview with a Professional:
Q&A
Joseph Martinez
Medical correspondence clerk, Westchester Medical
Group, White Plains, New York

Q: *How did you get started?*

A: When I started in 1999, I was working and taking classes at Bronx Community College. A friend of mine in college told me that the Westchester Medical Group was looking for someone in medical records and she said, "I thought about you."

I started as a clerk on the second floor. Then I moved along. I've had three positions since 1999. I started little by little. In my next position I was on switch board, trying to transfer all the phone calls through the whole facility. Now I'm a correspondence medical clerk. I answer the phone, I help the patients. I mail records. It's a more important position.

Q: *What's a typical day like?*

A: In the morning, when I get here at 7:30, the first thing that I do is walk all the way to the top on the third floor. I check my work. I check all my messages and call back everybody. I set up my computer. If I have to fax papers, I do that. If I have to send records, I do that.

I receive phone calls from different places. Insurance companies and medical offices call to ask for reports and records. Doctors' offices call and ask for reports or the status of a request. I can tell them if it's been mailed or if it's being processed.

I put my notes in the computer when I mail records. Everything is computerized now; we're trying to be paperless.

Q: *What's your advice for those starting a career?*

A: Whatever you want do, think about it first. If you think you'll be good at it, try to go for your dreams. If you like medical records, go for it. It's a multitask career, so it is enjoyable.

Q: *What's the best part about being a medical records technician?*

A: We normally have a processing time of two weeks. But if a person calls, and says: "I have an appointment tomorrow. I have something in my breast and I'm so scared. I know you have a processing time but I need my records right away," I enjoy processing their records right away. I feel like I help someone when I do their records when they need it. They say, "Thank you for helping me." That makes me feel good.

The Future

Technology is changing the way medical records technicians do their work. As more medical facilities rely on computers to store, analyze, and share records, information workers with high-tech skills and coding knowledge will be in great demand. Insurance companies' demands for more detail is also pushing the need for medical record technicians who compile and share health information that can often help a patient secure a much-needed appointment.

Did You Know?

The folks at Guinness World Records keep their own interesting medical records about unique medical cases—from the man who hiccuped the longest (68 years straight) to the man who had the most surgical operations (970!).

Job Seeking Tips

See the suggestions below and turn to Appendix A for advice on résumés, and interviews.

✔ Become certified in specific areas of the industry.

✔ Decide what you're interested in and seek relevant experience.

✔ Seek advice from the career placement office.

✔ Reach out to associations in your chosen field.

> **"One of the biggest challenges to medicine is the incorporation of information technology in our practices."**
> —Samuel Wilson, M.D., Deputy Director, National Institute of Environmental Health Sciences

Career Connections

For further information, contact the following organizations.

American Health Information Management Association http://www.ahima.org

National Cancer Registrars Association http://www.ncra-usa.org

Associate's Degree Programs

Here are a few schools offering quality medical records programs.

Hocking College, Nelsonville, Ohio

Indian River College, Fort Pierce, Florida

Louisiana State University at Eunice, Eunice, Louisiana

Turtle Mountain Community College, Belcourt, North Dakota

Vance-Granville Community College, Henderson, North Carolina

Financial Aid

Here are a few medical records scholarships. For more on financial aid turn to Appendix B.

The **Foundation of Research and Education (FORE)** of the AHIMA awards scholarships to AHIMA-member students enrolled in health information management programs.   http://www.ahima.org/fore

The **Jimmy Gamble Memorial Scholarship** is one of numerous memorial funds that provide scholarships to outstanding health information management students.   http://www.ahima.org/fore/contribute/scholmem.asp

Related Careers

Medical secretary, medical transcriptionist, and pharmacy technician.

Pharmacy Technician

Vital Statistics

Salary: The median wage for pharmacy technicians is about $11.40 an hour or about $24,000 a year, according to 2006 data from the U.S. Bureau of Labor Statistics.

Employment: The demand for skilled pharmacy technicians is high and is expected to continue to grow.

Education: Accredited programs in schools and pharmacies provide essential instruction and training for people who want to work as pharmacy technicians. When students finish their training, they can take a national exam for the Certified Pharmacy Technician (CPhT) credential, which can lead to better-paying jobs.

Work Environment: Pharmacy technicians work in well-lit, clean environments inside pharmacies in drugstores, grocery stories, discount stores, and hospitals.

We place a lot of trust in our pharmacies. When we pick up a prescription at a pharmacy, we're counting on it being exactly what the doctor ordered. At many pharmacies, pharmacy technicians help pharmacists fill these prescriptions. Working under the pharmacist's supervision, they check prescription requests for accuracy, mix and measure medicines, and label and price prescriptions. Misreading a prescription and giving someone the wrong drug or dosage isn't just an inconvenience; in some cases, such mistakes can be deadly. (If you ever see the film classic *It's A Wonderful Life,* the lead character—George Bailey—stops the local druggist from making just such a fatal error.)

Consequently, people who want to become pharmacy technicians must be precise, accurate workers who can handle stress. Because customers often don't feel well, and thus, are in no mood to wait, pharmacy technicians must also be fast workers who communicate well with others.

As a pharmacy technician, you help the pharmacist do his or her job. During the course of the day, you assist customers when they drop off or pick up prescriptions. You handle prescription requests called or faxed in from doctors' offices. You iron out insurance issues when insurers reject prescribed medications.

Of the 258,000 pharmacy technicians who work in the United States, about 70 percent work in retail pharmacies inside drugstores, grocery stores, department stores, and other retail outlets. About 20 percent work in hospitals, and a few are employed by Internet pharmacies, health clinics, wholesalers, and the federal government.

While requirements vary from state to state, the surest route to becoming a pharmacy technician involves training in a program that's been approved by the American Society of Health-System Pharmacists (http://www.ashp.org) or a regional or local accrediting board. You can find accredited programs at community colleges, trade schools, and even at some pharmacies.

Programs taught in schools that have been accredited by a respected accrediting agency, such as the Accrediting Commission of the National Association of Trade and Technical Schools (http://www.accsct.org) or the Accrediting Bureau of Health Education Schools (http://www.abhes.org) also are good bets.

The classroom instruction and clinical training you receive will prepare you to take an exam administered by the Pharmacy Technician Certification Board. Passing the exam will earn you Certified Pharmacy Technician (CPhT) credential—a title that will give you an edge in your job search.

Certified technicians earn the best wages in the field, as do those who garner extra pay by working evenings and weekends. In fact, the top 10 percent of pharmacy technicians make about $16.60 an hour.

Without a doubt, the job of a pharmacy technician, which is part retail, part health care, is stressful; but pharmacy technicians can take satisfaction in knowing their work helps customers feel better.

> **"I wanted to be a pharmacist. I liked the way our local pharmacist was always dressed in a nice white coat; he looked very calm, you'd give him money, and he'd give you something that you wanted to buy."**
> —Walter Matthau, actor

On the Job

As a pharmacy technician, your main job is to help the pharmacist do his job. In that role, you assist customers who need prescriptions filled. You also handle prescription requests from doctors' offices. Once you have the prescription, you verify the information, making sure it's accurate and complete. Depending on the prescribed medicine, you may also count, pour, weigh, measure, or mix it. You then pick a container for the medicine, label and price it, and record the prescription in the pharmacy's records. The pharmacist will check the prescription, and once he or she has approved it, you can give it to the customer.

As a pharmacy technician, you also help keep patient records, prepare insurance forms, answer phones, and take inventory of prescriptions and over-the-counter medications. Pharmacy technicians also often play a key role in helping untangle the mysteries of insurance, troubleshooting claims so customers are able to get the medicine they need.

In hospitals, nursing homes, and assisted-living facilities, pharmacy techs prepare and deliver medicine to patients. They copy the information about each medicine into a patient's profile, and assemble a 24-hour supply of medicine for each patient. The packages, which are separated and labeled for each dosage, are placed on each patient's medicine cabinet, so the supervising pharmacist can double-check them.

 ## Keys to Success

To be a successful pharmacy technician, you need
- math and computer skills
- good organization
- knowledge of medications
- typing ability
- precision
- strong communication skills
- courteous manner
- no history of drug or substance abuse

Do You Have What It Takes?

To work as a pharmacy technician, you need to be a detail-oriented person who can quickly compute dosages and accurately record prescriptions. Because the medications you're putting together are often life-and-death matters, you must be a careful, precise worker who appreciates the magnitude of your duties.

A Typical Day at Work

Pharmacy technicians work in well-lit, clean work areas. They spend much of the workday standing and may need to lift heavy boxes or climb up on ladders to reach supplies on high shelves. Part of their day is spent handling calls and visits from customers and sometimes speaking to physicians about prescriptions that need to be filled. Depending on the pharmacy's hours, some pharmacy techs may be required to work at night and on weekends and holidays.

How to Break In

While in high school, you can get a jump on your career by taking courses in chemistry, English, and health. You also can pick up experience by volunteering at a hospital, or working part time as a cashier or aide at a local pharmacy or drugstore. In fact, some large retail employers provide in-house training and educational funding for promising employees interested in working in the pharmacy field.

Once you complete your training, you'll be eligible to take a certification exam administered by the Pharmacy Technician Certification Board. While not mandatory in all states, passing the test shows potential employers that you've mastered the skills needed to do the job well.

Two-Year Training

Enrolling in a pharmacy tech program at an accredited school or even at an accredited pharmacy will prepare you to work in this field. During school, your instruction will focus on medical terminology, specialized calculations, and record keeping. You'll learn about basic pharmacology, the fundamentals of disease, basic microbiology, and therapeutic agents. You'll study legal and ethical topics related to pharmacology. Depending on your computer skills, you may need to take courses that teach you how to work with Microsoft Word and Excel. As part of your instruction at many schools, you'll also have a chance to gain on-the-job experience as an intern at a pharmacy.

When you finish your training, you'll be ready to take the National Pharmacy Technician Certification Exam, given by the Pharmacy Technician Certification Board. Because of the continuing advances in medicines, you'll need to continue your education throughout your career. In fact, technicians must complete 20 hours of additional training every two years to qualify for recertification.

What to Look For in a School

When considering a two-year school, be sure to ask these questions:

☞ Does the school offer work-related courses that will teach you how to fill prescriptions, work with insurance companies, and deal with customers?

☞ Is the program accredited by the American Society of Health-System Pharmacists (http://www.ashp.org) or a regional or local accrediting agency? Or is the program taught at a school that's been accredited by a respected accrediting agency, such as the Accrediting Commission of

the National Association of Trade and Technical Schools (http://www
.accsct.org) or the Accrediting Bureau of Health Education Schools
(http://www.abhes.org)?

☞ Does the school have contacts to help students receive on-the-job
training in formal internship programs?

☞ What is the school's job placement rate?

☞ Will the program prepare you to take and pass the certification exam
in your field?

☞ What are the instructors' credentials? Have they worked in the
industry? Have they kept up with new techniques and procedures
in the industry? Are they available outside the classroom?

☞ Do the classrooms and labs have up-to-date equipment?

The Future

An aging population needs more health care, creating a growing demand
for pharmacy technicians who can help pharmacists quickly and accurately
fill prescriptions. Most pharmacy technicians currently work in retail pharmacies. As more patients rely on the Internet for prescriptions, Internet
pharmacies could very well provide pharmacy techs with additional job
opportunities. Pharmacy techs who are certified and stay abreast of technical advances will fare best. For example, robotic machines that dispense
medicines are becoming more common. Techs who know how to work
these machines will have an advantage over those who don't.

Did You Know?

Coca Cola was created by a pharmacist from Atlanta, Georgia. John Stith
Pemberton created the fizzy soda, now commonly referred to as "Coke," in
the late 1800s.

Job Seeking Tips

See the suggestions below and turn to Appendix A for advice on résumés,
and interviews.

✔ Become certified in specific areas of the industry.

✔ Decide what you're interested in and seek relevant experience.

✔ Seek advice from the career placement office.

✔ Reach out to associations in your chosen field.

Interview with a Professional:
Q & A

Pam Ledford

Certified pharmacy technician, Midway Park Pharmacy,
Lancaster, Texas

Q: *How did you get started?*

A: I got started with Revco Discount Drug Stores. I got started by being a floor manager. I started working myself into pharmacy: That was a big interesting part of the store that I wanted to find out more about. The pharmacist started showing me different things.

Revco was bought out by Eckerds, and then I started working at Eckerds as a drug clerk. They started training me as a pharmacy-tech-in-training. I took a pharmacy tech prep course and then I passed the exam in 2000 to become certified as a pharmacy technician.

Q: *What's a typical day like?*

A: I fill prescriptions. While the phone is ringing, I have people waiting for their prescriptions. It's chaotic. I work normally Mondays through Fridays from 9 to 6. I occasionally work on Saturdays.

I come in and check the fax machines to see if any refill requests have been sent to us. I do data entry of the refill requests that have been approved.

We have a folder of medications that are on order, and I fill those. In between that, I answer the phone and wait on people who come in. I also call insurance companies if there's a prescription the insurance company is rejecting for some reason.

Q: *What's your advice for those starting a career?*

A: Hang in there. It's not going to be great every day. There are always going to be problems. A lot of times, there will be things that pop up that you can't handle. Go to the pharmacist and have him help you. My best advice is hang in there, and it will be rewarding.

Q: *What's the best part about being a pharmacy technician?*

A: When people come into the pharmacy, we help them feel better by doing the prescription as fast as we can. Also, teamwork: We're not just designated to do just one job. We're cross-trained and we help each other to make the day go better.

Career Connections

For further information, contact the following organizations.

Accreditation Council for Pharmacy Education http://www
.acpe-accredit.org

American Society of Health-System Pharmacists http://www.ashp.org

National Pharmacy Technician Association http://www
.pharmacytechnician.org

Pharmacy Technician Certification Board http://www.ptcb.org

Associate's Degree Programs

Here are a few schools offering quality pharmacy technician programs.

Jones County Junior College, Ellisville, Mississippi

Malcolm X College, Chicago, Illinois

Spokane Community College, Spokane, Washington

Trident Technical College, Charleston, South Carolina

Financial Aid

Here are a few pharmacy technician scholarships. For more on financial aid, see Appendix B.

Walgreens provides financial assistance to employees pursuing pharmacy careers. http://www.walgreens.com/about/careers/pharmacy/eduassistprg.jsp

The **Pharmacy Technology Scholarship** goes to in-state pharmacy tech students at Durham Technical Community College in Durham, North Carolina. http://www.durhamtech.org/html/prospective/scholarshipsfall.htm

Related Careers

Pharmacy aide, dental assistant, licensed practical nurse, licensed vocational nurse, medical records technician, occupational therapy assistant, physical therapist assistant, and surgical assistant.

Medical Assistant/ Physician Assistant

Vital Statistics

Salary: The median annual wage for medical assistants is about $24,600, and for physician assistants, it's about $69,400, according to 2006 figures from the U.S. Bureau of Labor Statistics.

Employment: The demand for medical assistants and physician assistants is expected to continue to be strong, especially in rural and inner-city clinics.

Education: Accredited schools provide essential instruction and training for people who want to work as medical assistants and physician assistants.

Work Environment: Medical assistants and physician assistants work in hospitals, doctor's offices, medical clinics, and other health care facilities.

Medical assistants do just what their job title implies: They offer assistance that helps medical practices run more smoothly. Under the supervision of a doctor, they answer phones, schedule appointments, and call in prescriptions. Medical assistants also help out with clinical tasks, which can vary from state to state. Depending on where they work, they may assist a physician during an exam, explain treatments to a patient, administer prescribed medications, and call in drug refills.

Like medical assistants, physician assistants work under the supervision of a doctor, but because of their additional medical training, they are given more responsibilities. They can examine and treat patients, order and interpret lab tests, and make diagnoses. Physician assistants, or PAs, can also suture cuts, and put splints or casts on minor injuries. In many states, they can prescribe medicines.

About 387,000 medical assistants work in the United States. Of those, about 60 percent work in doctors' offices. They also work in hospitals, outpatient health care centers, and nursing homes. Like doctors, some specialize and work primarily in pediatrics, internal medicine, and other medical areas. About 62,000 jobs are held by physician assistants, with about 15 percent working more than one job. All the hard work has its rewards: The top-earning physician assistants make about $94,900 a year, while the best-paid medical assistants make about $34,700 a year.

You can obtain the training needed to work as a medical assistant or physician assistant at numerous accredited schools throughout the United States. Students enrolled in a medical assistant's program can complete their initial training in just a year. Those who want to pursue an associate's degree can finish their studies in two years. During school, you'll take medical and business-office courses. You'll also receive on-the-job training as an intern in a doctor's office, a hospital, or other health care facility.

> **"Once you get started in health care, you'd better watch out because it's addictive, and makes you want to stay. It fulfills a need in us because we're making a difference; we're able to help."**
> —Rebecca Walker, certified medical assistant

On the Job

Medical assistants help keep a doctor's office or medical clinic running smoothly. They answer phones, greet patients, update medical records, fill out insurance forms, schedule appointments, set up lab services, and handle bills. Depending on their state's regulations, medical assistants also take medical histories, record vital signs, explain treatment procedures to patients, prepare patients for the exam, and assist the doctor during exams.

In some offices, medical assistants collect and prepare lab specimens, sterilize medical instruments, and prepare and give prescribed medications to patients. They also draw blood, telephone prescriptions to a pharmacy, prepare patients for X-rays, remove sutures, and change dressings.

Physician assistants perform many of the same procedures as medical assistants, and also perform routine tasks that might normally be done by a doctor. For instance, they can examine and treat patients, order and read X-rays, and in some states, prescribe medicines

Keys to Success

To be a successful medical assistant or physician assistant, you need
- patience
- good communication skills
- office skills
- manual dexterity
- a calm, gentle manner
- math and computer skills
- medical knowledge

Do You Have What It Takes?

To work as a medical assistant or a physician assistant, you must be a team player who works well with physicians, nurses, and other medical care professionals, and communicates well with patients. For those interested in the field of medicine, the career can be ideal as it gives you the chance to assume many of the responsibilities of a physician and see what the career is like up close. Also, if you like the challenges of multitasking, this could be a job that matches your abilities and interests.

A Typical Day at Work

Medical assistants and physician assistants work in doctors' offices, medical clinics, hospitals, and other health care facilities. They often work 40-hour weeks. Depending on the medical facility's hours, they may need to work nights or weekends. No day is typical as activities change from day to day. One day, you can be helping a doctor with patients all day; the next day, you might be attending to paperwork.

How to Break In

While in high school, you can get a jump on your career by taking as many courses in science and math as you can. You also can volunteer or seek a part-time job in a doctor's office, medical clinic, or hospital. Once you enroll in a college program, be sure to become an active student member of professional associations, such as the American Association of Medical Assistants or the American Academy of Physician Assistants. Such organizations can provide you with mentors, job leads, and career advice.

When you finish your schooling, take the time to become certified in your field. To become a certified medical assistant, you'll need to pass an exam administered by the America Association of Medical Assistants. You also can seek certification from other professional organizations, including the American Society of Podiatric Medical Assistants and the Allied Health Personnel in Ophthalmology. While not mandatory, gaining certification(s) in your field shows prospective employers that you know what you're doing.

To become a certified physician assistant, you need to pass the Physician Assistant National Certifying Examination, which is administered by the National Commission on Certification of Physician Assistants (NCCPA).

Two-Year Training

Universities, colleges, trade schools, and even hospitals offer educational and training programs for people who want to become medical assistants and physician assistants. You can often wrap up the training needed to work as a medical assistant in as little as one year. Those who want to pursue an associate's degree can generally finish their course work in two years.

Students enrolled in an accredited medical assistant program will learn about medicine in courses such as anatomy and physiology, while also mastering practical subjects, such as office skills, medical law, and patient relations. They will also have a chance to work as an intern in a doctor's office, a hospital, or other medical care facility.

Because a physician assistant has medical responsibilities, the education and training requirements tend to be more stringent. While a few programs can be completed with a two-year associate's degree, most programs typically require students to have already completed at least two years of college and have work experience in the health field. Completion of these programs often results in a bachelor's or master's degree.

While in school, you'll take classes in health-related subjects, such as human anatomy, physiology, disease prevention, and medical ethics. You'll also receive clinical training in different medical specialties, including internal medicine, geriatrics, emergency medicine, and pediatrics. The good news is that PA students often work under the supervision of doctors who are looking to hire PAs. Do good work, and you could end up with a job when your training ends.

Your education and training will prepare you to take the Physician Assistant National Certifying Examination. Pass the test and you can officially claim to be a physician assistant–certified.

What to Look For in a School

When considering a two-year school, be sure to ask these questions:

☞ Does the school offer work-related courses that will teach you to assist a doctor in a medical setting?

☞ Is the school accredited by professional organizations, such as the Commission on Accreditation of Allied Health Education Programs, the Accrediting Bureau of Health Education Schools, or the American Academy of Physician Assistants?

☞ Does the school have the connections to successfully place students in clinical training rotations at medical facilities?

☞ What is the school's job placement rate?

☞ Will the program prepare you to pass certification exams in your field?

☞ What are the instructors' credentials? Have they worked in the industry? Have they kept up with new techniques and procedures in the industry? Are they available outside the classroom?

☞ Do the classrooms and labs have up-to-date equipment?

Interview with a Professional:
Q & A

Rebecca Walker

Certified medical assistant, Albemarle Area Urology,
Elizabeth City, North Carolina

Q: *How did you get started?*

A: I started working in a physician's office in an administrative capacity and became interested in becoming a medical assistant. I reached out to the local chapter of American Association of Medical Assistants. They explained that a medical assistant is someone who is trained to do everything in a physician's office from paperwork to clinical duties. We answer the phone, pay bills, and even do maintenance if we need to. We take patients back, we take temperatures, we take blood pressures, we sterilize equipment. I studied for the exam and took it.

There is always something new, something challenging. I enjoy the contact in health care with the patients. I also enjoy the administrative aspects of the paperwork. The physicians that I've worked with have always been very interested and willing to teach, so you learn something while working with them all the time.

Q: *What's a typical day like?*

A: We start out early in the morning. We usually get here about 30 minutes ahead of time to make sure the office is open and ready to receive patients.

When the physician is here and seeing patients, it's busy. The phone is ringing. The patients are coming and going. Each day is kind of different. You never know when the patient comes through the door what will happen.

During the course of the day, I work mainly in the administrative part. I help answer phones. I answer questions patients might have about insurance or billing. I'm the backup for the front desk person, the one who checks patients in, checks patients out, and schedules X-rays and tests they might need done.

In the administrative area, we're mostly concerned with paper. That includes everything from patient charts and making sure they're ready for the next day to filing insurance claims, which is done electronically.

There's a lot involved: Have we sent out the bills? Are there patients who need to have reminders sent to them to make an appointment? Have we contacted insurance companies for patients who are scheduled for surgery?

(continued on next page)

(continued from previous page)

Q: *What's your advice for those starting a career?*

A: Seek out an accredited medical assistant program. Enroll in the program and take the certification exam to be certified. That credential tells the physician who is looking to employ someone that this medical assistant is concerned and wants to make sure to do the best possible job.

Once you become credentialed, keep up with your education. The nice thing about certification is we have to recertify every five years, and keep up with the current education.

Q: *What's the best part about being a medical assistant?*

A: I'm helping the physician see the patients in the most efficient way possible so that all he has to do is concentrate on taking care of his patients, so he doesn't have to worry about the details: is the room fully stocked with everything he needs? Everything is done to make sure the physician is able to see the patient and render the quality that he'd like to provide, and thereby you're helping the patient receive the best medical care.

The Future

Pressures to keep medical costs down will create a growing demand for physician assistants and medical assistants, who can lighten doctors' workload and help medical offices run more efficiently. Advances in technology that allow doctors to view what's going on from afar will create more opportunities for physician assistants and medical assistants to work in remote areas that doctors can't easily reach in person.

Did You Know?

Actor Todd Louiso played an uptight and conscientious medical assistant in a recurring role on the CBS medical drama, *Chicago Hope*.

Job Seeking Tips

See the suggestions below and turn to Appendix A for advice on résumés, and interviews.

✔ Become certified in your field and/or specialty.

✔ Decide what you're interested in and seek relevant experience.

✔ Seek advice from the career placement office.

✔ Reach out to associations in your chosen field.

Career Connections

For further information, contact the following organizations.

Accrediting Bureau of Health Education Schools   http://www
.abhes.org

American Academy of Physician Assistants (AAPA)   http://www
.aapa.org

The American Association of Medical Assistants   http://www
.aama-ntl.org

**Commission on Accreditation of Allied Health Education
Programs** http://www.caahep.org

National Commission on Certification of Physician Assistants
http://www.nccpa.net

Physician Assistant Education Association   http://www
.paeaonline.org

Associate's Degree Programs

Here are a few schools offering quality physician assistant and/or medical
assistant programs.

Arkansas Tech University, Russellville, Arkansas

Capital Community College, Hartford, Connecticut

Cuyahoga Community College, Cleveland, Ohio

Riverside Community College, Riverside, California

Financial Aid

Here are a few medical assistant and/or physician assistant scholarships.
For more on financial aid, turn to Appendix B.

The **FA Davis Student Award** goes to a student enrolled in a CAAHEP-
accredited medical assisting program who creates a winning ad pro-
moting the profession.   http://www.apta.org/AM/Template
.cfm?Section=Home&CONTENTID=33938&TEMPLATE=/CM/Content
Display.cfm

The **PA Foundation Scholarship Program** awards scholarships to
AAPA student members in accredited PA programs.   http://www
.saaapa.aapa.org/resources/pafscholarship.htm

Related Careers

Audiologist, occupational therapist, physical therapist, registered nurse, and speech-language pathologist.

Veterinary Technician

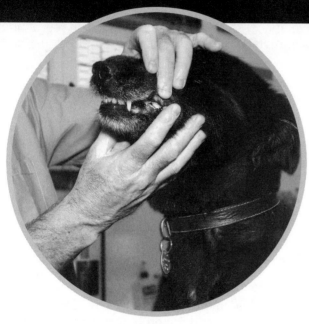

Vital Statistics

Salary: Veterinary technologists and technicians earn a median $12 an hour, or about $25,000 a year, according to 2006 figures from the U. S. Bureau of Labor Statistics.

Employment: The demand for skilled veterinary technicians is high and is expected to continue to grow.

Education: Accredited schools and clinical training under the supervision of a veterinarian provide essential instruction for people who want to work as a veterinary technician.

Work Environment: Veterinary technicians usually work with vets at animal clinics and animal hospitals. Some also work in zoos, pet stores, animal shelters, and other locales that house or care for animals.

Do you think you can make a cat say, "Ahh?" If you have a way with animals, a career as a veterinary tech can be an ideal job. A veterinary technician does the same work as a nurse. Only instead of helping a doctor care for human patients, a veterinary technician helps a veterinary care for animal patients—dogs, cats, birds, horses, and even more exotic animals such as snakes and weasels. When an owner brings a pet in for treatment, the vet tech gathers information about the animal's medical history and records the data. Depending on what the animal needs, the tech may give it a shot, take an X-ray, collect a blood sample, or prepare an animal for surgery.

Besides caring for the animals that come in, vet techs help the pets' owners. A vet tech may give an owner advice on how to feed an animal, show how to change a bandage, or offer consolation when an animal dies.

A two-year accredited veterinary technician program can provide you with the skills needed to work in this field. Not only will you have classroom work but you'll eventually have an opportunity to receive clinical training under the watchful eye of a veterinarian. To become a licensed vet technician, you'll need to meet your state's requirements. In most states, you must graduate from an accredited two-year veterinary technician program, successfully complete clinical training in a veterinary practice, and pass the National Veterinary Technician (NVT) exam or a similar exam administered by individual states. To work as a veterinary technologist, you generally need to complete a four-year degree, complete the required clinical training, and pass a certification exam.

About 60,000 veterinary technicians and technologists work in the United States. Most veterinary technicians start their careers in veterinary practices; but other opportunities exist. A skilled veterinary tech, for example, can work as a researcher in a biomedical lab, care for animals in a zoo or wildlife facility, or work as a sales rep for a veterinary supply company.

On the Job

Veterinary technicians help vets diagnose and treat medical conditions in animals. They collect blood and urine for lab tests, clean an animal's teeth, and prepare tissue samples. They also record an animal's health history, take and record X-rays, and offer advice to owners about animal care. Veterinary technicians often have to hold or restrain an animal while it's being treated, and run the risk of being bitten or scratched by an unhappy patient.

Some veterinary technicians specialize in treating large animals, such as cows and horses. In that role, a vet tech may be asked to go to the ranch to care for an injured horse or vaccinate cows. When an animal is seriously injured or ill, vet techs sometimes have to euthanize it, which can be especially tough because people who go into this field generally love animals.

**"The best doctor in the world is a veterinarian.
He can't ask his patients what is the matter.
He's got to just know."**
—Will Rogers, humorist

Keys to Success

To be a successful veterinary technician, you need
- patience
- good communication skills
- office skills
- manual dexterity
- a calm, gentle manner
- math and computer skills
- a love of animals

Do You Have What It Takes?

To work as a veterinary technician, you must be able to work well with animals as well as their owners, who often seek your guidance and comfort. You need to be emotionally strong enough to work with animals that are sick and will sometimes need to be put to sleep. An interest in science and medicine is essential as well.

A Typical Day at Work

Veterinary technicians work with animals in vet offices, animal clinics, shelters, zoos, and other locales. Vet technicians often work 40 to 50 hours a week. Those who work in shelters or animal hospitals may need to be on duty 24 hours a day or work overnight shifts. A typical day at work is often similar to one at a doctor's office. Patients get checked in and examined. Some patients, though, must be kept overnight. Sometimes you have to shave part of the animal to give an injection of medicine or hook an animal up to an IV to receive fluids. Keeping records on the animal's condition, progress, and medical history comes with the job.

How to Break In

You can get a jump on your career while in high school by taking courses in math, science, biology, health, and computers. High school is a good time to volunteer at an animal shelter. You may even be able to land a part-time job in a vet's office or kennel, where you can answer phones, file records, clean cages, and perform other basic duties.

While in college, be sure to become an active student member of professional associations, such as the National Association of Veterinary Technicians in America (NAVTA). Doing so will give you a chance to meet others in your field and also give you access to job listings, career advice, and other helpful information.

Two-Year Training

Enrolling in an accredited veterinary program can prepare you for a career in this field. The American Veterinary Medical Association has accredited more than 120 two-year veterinary technician programs, plus about 15 four-year veterinary technology programs and a handful of online offerings for those who don't live near a school that offers a program.

During school, you'll take classes in which you'll learn about medical terminology, animal anatomy, and animal nutrition. You'll also learn about technical treatments, surgical prep, medicine, and anesthesia. You'll learn how to help give a physical exam, collect information about a patient, care for a hospitalized animal, and clean a pet's teeth. You will begin to take and read X-rays and assist a vet during surgery. Part of your educational training will include clinical experience in a veterinary practice. This hands-on training is often referred to as a *practicum* or *externship*, and is an essential part of your schooling.

While the specifics for licensing vary from state to state, most states require veterinary techs to pass a National Veterinary Technician (NVT) exam or a similar exam administered by individual states. Veterinary technicians who want to specialize can also take exams to become credentialed or certified in specific areas, such as emergency care, research, and dental care.

What to Look For in a School

When considering a two-year school, be sure to ask these questions:

☞ Does the school offer work-related courses?

☞ Is the school accredited by the American Veterinary Medical Association?

☞ Does the school have contacts to help students obtain clinical training at veterinary practices?

☞ What is the school's job placement rate?

☞ Will the program prepare you to take and pass certification exams in your field or specialty?

☞ What are the instructors' credentials? Have they worked in the industry? Have they kept up with new techniques and procedures in the industry? Are they available outside the classroom?

☞ Do the classrooms and labs have up-to-date equipment?

The Future

Pet owners who are willing to pay for advanced care are creating a growing need for skilled veterinary technicians. Veterinary technicians who specialize in areas such as preventive dental care and surgical procedures will be in especially high demand. Vet techs will also be needed to work in other areas, including shelters, wildlife facilities, diagnostic labs, and food safety inspection.

Did You Know?

Never give your cat aspirin, unless advised to do so by your vet. Aspirin can cause hemorrhaging in the gastrointestinal tract. It can also depress bone marrow activity, slowing the production of red blood cells, and may also damage the kidneys.

Interview with a Professional:
Q&A

Rebecca Rose

Certified veterinary technician, Gunnison, Colorado

Q: *How did you get started?*

A: I always wanted to be a veterinary technician. My mother worked for a veterinary in the early 1970s. She was secretary/veterinary assistant. I would go in to help her out. I would hang out and pet the dogs as any 10-year-old wants to do. I've known this is what I wanted to do since I was 10.

Q: *What's a typical day like?*

A: You put in long days. When I managed a vet clinic, I suggested we schedule our vet techs for four 10-hour days. You're coming in at 7:30 in the morning and leaving around 6:30. A typical day for a veterinary technician in a veterinary hospital starts early in the morning. I love to do surgery, so I focused my work with a surgical vet. I'd get myself prepped for the surgeries for the day. As the animals arrived, I'd talk to the owners, explain the procedures, and explain some of the postoperative care that would follow.

During the day, I would answer any of their questions and relieve any concerns they might have about the procedures and about their pets being with us that day. The vet would prepare himself for surgery. We would anesthetize the animal. Then I would help with the surgery. During postoperative care, I would make sure the animal is recovering. I would take his temperature and check his pulse rate. I would update the charts and follow up with the vet. I would write in the records all the anesthetics and drugs we used.

Then later on, we'd call the owner and let him know what's going on with his or her pet. It helps relieve some of the anxiety that's going on with having a pet in surgery.

As a vet tech doing large animal work, you will have lots of variables. You could do artificial insemination of a horse. You could do an ultrasound of a horse to see if it's pregnant. You do X-rays all the time of horses' feet. Horses tend to go through fences and get cut up so, so you could do a lot of suturing. You might go out and work with cattle and vaccinate them.

Q: *What's your advice for those starting a career?*

A: Complete that two-year program and take the National veterinary Tech Exam. That way you can get credentialed in the state where you work.

Follow your passion. I always explain to my technicians, you have to enjoy what you're doing. If you're passionate about large animals, do large animals. If you're passionate about oncology, and helping people with the transition of animals later in life, do oncology. There are numerous options within vet technology. You can work through the academy and become specialized in dentistry, emergency, critical care, and animal behaviors.

Q: *What's the best part about being a medical assistant?*

A: I love it all. I love dealing with the people. Yes, you deal with the animals but you have their owners as well. You need to be a well-rounded person in that you need to be able to relate to the owners.

I enjoy working with the people in veterinary medicine. They're fabulous. They're dedicated to animals that aren't able to speak to them verbally. You have to have a special connection with those animals to understand where their pain is and how to help them. It's like dealing with a five-year-old. It's a puzzle.

Job Seeking Tips

See the suggestions below and turn to Appendix A for advice on résumés, and interviews.

✔ Become certified in specific areas of the industry.

✔ Decide what you're interested in and seek relevant experience.

✔ Seek advice from the career placement office.

✔ Reach out to associations in your chosen field.

Career Connections

For further information, contact the following organizations.

Academy of Veterinary Dental Technicians http://www.avdt.us

Academy of Veterinary Emergency & Critical Care Technicians http://www.avecct.org

American Animal Hospital Association http://www.aahanet.org

American Association for Laboratory Animal Science http://www.aalas.org

American Veterinary Medical Association http://www.avma.org

National Association of Veterinary Technicians in America http://www.navta.net

Society of Veterinary Behavior Technicians http://www.svbt.org

Associate's Degree Programs

Here are a few schools offering quality veterinary technician programs.

Brevard Community College, Cocoa, Florida

Camden County College, Blackwood, New Jersey

Gwinnett Technical College, Lawrenceville, Georgia

Wayne County Community College District, Detroit, Michigan

Yuba College, Marysville, California

Financial Aid

Here are a few scholarships for veterinary technician programs. For more on financial aid, turn to Appendix B.

American Kennel Club/Hartz Mountain Corporation Veterinary Technician Student Scholarships go to full-time students enrolled in an accredited vet program and who are members of NAVTA. http://www.akc.org/vetoutreach

The **National Association of Veterinary Technicians in America** offers scholarships to members of its organization enrolled in accredited programs.   http://www.navta.net

Related Careers

Animal care worker, animal service worker, veterinary assistant, veterinary technician, and veterinarian.

Speech-Language Pathology Assistant

> **Vital Statistics**
>
> **Salary:** Speech-language pathology assistants have an estimated median salary in the $30,000 range, based on a comparison of 2006 salaries for similar positions in related fields.
>
> **Employment:** The demand for skilled speech-language pathology assistants (SLPAs) is high, and expected to continue to grow.
>
> **Education:** A two-year degree in a speech-language pathology program coupled with fieldwork can prepare you for a career as an SLPA.
>
> **Work Environment:** Depending on the job assignment, an SLPA works in hospitals, nursing homes, rehab centers, day-care centers, schools, and patients' homes.

Talk is something many people take for granted. We babble as babies, start saying a few words as toddlers, and eventually piece together eloquent sentences. However, for some people, speaking clearly requires months and even years of speech therapy. Whether it's a child who struggles to say certain sounds or a stroke victim who has to learn to talk again, speech therapy provided by speech therapists and their assistants can dramatically improve lives.

Speech therapists, or speech-language pathologists (SLPs), first diagnose the problem and prescribe a course of action to help a patient improve his or her speech. They, along with SLPAs, then use a variety of treatments and therapies to help patients communicate more clearly.

As an occupation, the SLPA is relatively new. The use of SLPAs was first approved by many states in the 1970s. To help ensure quality treatment, the American Speech-Language-Hearing Association (ASHA) has created guidelines that spell out what assistants can and can't do. For example, assistants can't perform diagnostic tests or make referrals for additional service. However, they can carry out prescribed treatments and therapies. Depending on a patient's needs, an assistant might help a patient do drills to improve pronunciation of problematic sounds, have a preschooler drink yogurt from a tiny straw to build up the oral muscles needed to talk, or help school children understand concepts, such as "on" and "under." While working with a patient, an assistant keeps notes on a patient's progress and shares the findings with the supervising therapist.

A growing push to cut medical costs, coupled with an aging baby-boom population who may suffer speech-related problems after strokes and other health problems, is expected to fuel the demand for assistants, who can provide needed therapy for less money than full-fledged therapists.

An associate's degree in a technical program that focuses on speech therapy can prepare you to work as a speech therapy assistant. Just be aware that licensing requirements—and job titles—vary from state to state. Depending on where you live, you may be employed as an SLP assistant, an SLP aide, a paraprofessional, a special education teacher assistant, a communication aide, or a service extender.

The median salary for an SLPA involves a bit of guesswork. The American Speech-Language-Hearing Association, which doesn't track salaries for SLPAs, notes that assistants in similar fields, such as occupational therapy and physical therapy, generally earn about 60 to 75 percent of their professional counterparts. Based on that thinking and a median annual salary of $52,600 for an SLP, an SLPA's median salary would probably be in the $30,000 range.

On the Job

An SPLA works closely with a patient's speech therapist. During a patient's screening or evaluation, the SLPA often assists the speech therapist by taking notes or setting up the equipment. After the speech therapist has prescribed a treatment plan, an SLPA can follow the prescribed plan to help patients overcome voice, fluency, articulation, or hearing problems. The SLPA can, for example, guide an adult through drills to improve the patient's pronunciation, play games with a child to help him or her grasp concepts such as "up" or "down," or help a child improve oral muscle strength by having the child blow through a special whistle.

When an assistant isn't working with a patient, he or she still has plenty of work to do: The SLPA often needs to prepare materials for future sessions, schedule prescribed treatments, and update reports on a patient's progress.

Keys to Success

To be a successful speech-language pathology assistant, you need

- patience
- strong communication skills
- motivational skills
- problem-solving abilities
- teamwork skills
- attention to detail

Do You Have What It Takes?

To work as an SLPA, you need to be a team player, one who can take directions from the supervising SLP and explain the therapy to the patient and his or her family. Being creative and upbeat will help you keep the therapy fun, and hold the patient's interest. Therapy can take a long time to kick in, so patience is vital. An interest in speech and communications is also a plus.

A Typical Day at Work

As an SLPA, your workday revolves around your patients. If you treat schoolchildren, you'll work with them at a table or desk during the school day. If you work with stroke patients, you will give them therapy in hospital rooms or rehab centers. You start a typical day helping a pathologist with a child who is having trouble pronouncing letters. The rhythm of his speech is off and he also has a slight stutter. Based on his speech impairment, you and the pathologist develop a plan of exercises to help the child improve his speech. In the afternoon, you visit with a stroke victim who is having oral motor problems that are giving her difficulties eating and swallowing.

How to Break In

You can get a jump on your career plans while in high school by taking courses in health, biology, language arts, math, computer science, and foreign languages. Now's a good time to develop strong skills in reading, writing, speaking and listening, which you'll need once you start working as an SLPA.

When you're in college in an SLPA program, you'll have a chance to gain experience in the field under the supervision of a seasoned SLP. Sign up for as many hours as you can, and in a variety of settings. Doing so will give you an edge once you start looking for a job.

While in school, you also should become a student member of professional associations, such as the ASHA. Not only will these organizations give you a chance to meet others in your chosen field, but they can provide helpful information on schools, scholarships, and job openings.

Two-Year Training

During school, you'll take academic courses such as psychology, sociology, and composition, which will give you a strong foundation for working and communicating with a diverse population. You'll also take courses directly related to speech pathology. You may, for example, take "Introduction to Behavior Management," "Applied Phonetics for SLPA" and "Language Theory and Treatment for the SLPA." You'll also be given a chance to work in the field under the supervision of an experienced SLP. In fact, the ASHA recommends that students receive 100 hours of field training.

What to Look For in a School

When considering a two-year school, be sure to ask these questions:

☞ Does the school offer work-related courses that will prepare you to work as a speech-language pathology assistant?

☞ Does the school follow guidelines established by the ASHA?

☞ What is the school's job placement rate?

☞ Does the school provide you with a chance to receive training in the field under the supervision of a certified speech therapist?

☞ What are the instructors' credentials? Have they worked in the industry? Have they kept up with new techniques and procedures in the industry? Are they available outside the classroom?

The Future

A push to cut medical costs coupled with an aging population's need for speech therapy will create a need for more SLPAs who can provide many of the same services as an SLP, at a reduced cost.

> ## "Speech is power: speech is to persuade, to convert, to compel."
> —Ralph Waldo Emerson, essayist and poet

Did You Know?

Samuel L. Jackson tried out for his first acting role on the advice of a speech therapist, who thought it would help him overcome a stuttering problem. Not only did the "therapy" work, but Jackson went on to become a major box-office star in movies such as *Pulp Fiction* and *Shaft*.

Interview with a Professional:
Q&A

Rebecca Pope

Speech and language pathology assistant, Bonita
United School District, San Dimas, California

Q: *How did you get started?*

A: I wanted a career change. I was a factory worker. I registered at Pasadena City College for an introductory course in the speech-language pathology assistant program, and I was hooked. I went through the program and found it was my calling.

Q: *What's a typical day like?*

A: I see about six groups of kids a day. Each session lasts half an hour. Then, as soon as school is out, we don't go home. We do paperwork and prepare for the next day.

I currently go to four different schools. If the kids are working on a sound, say, they need to work on "r," I have some kind of activity to help them get the placement for that. I try to be creative and have lots of things for them to do, so that they're not getting bored.

A lot of kids don't get the concept of a preposition, like "put it *on* a table." They don't have a clue about what "on" or "under" mean. We do activities that let them put something on the table again and again, until they say, "Oh, that's what it means!"

Q: *What's your advice for those starting a career?*

A: Make your own [speech therapy] materials. It brings life to what you're doing.

We sell ourselves short when we take the easy road and take something off the shelf that we bought. When I made my own materials, I saw new opportunities and it gave me new ideas and helped me grow. My imagination just took off.

Q: *What's the best part about being an SLPA?*

A: Seeing the kids get it. There is nothing more rewarding for me than to have a child finally be able to say that sound or get that concept and connect the dots. You can see that light going on. It's so rewarding to see them get it. They feel so good about themselves. You feel like you're accomplishing something. You're changing their lives.

I felt the same when I was working with stroke patients. They desperately wanted to reclaim their lives. There's nothing more rewarding for me. That's why I'm in it. I always feel good at the end of the day.

Job Seeking Tips

See the suggestions below and turn to Appendix A for advice on résumés, and interviews.

✔ Decide what you're interested in and seek relevant experience.

✔ Seek advice from the career placement office.

✔ Reach out to associations in your chosen field.

Career Connections

For further information, contact the following organizations.

American Speech-Language-Hearing Association (ASHA) http://www.asha.org

American Speech-Language Hearing Foundation http://www.ashfoundation.org/foundation

Speech-Pathology http://www.speech-pathology.org

Associate's Degree Programs

Here are a few schools offering quality speech-language pathology assistant programs:

Elms College, Chicopee, Massachusetts

Lake Land College, Mattoon, Illinois

Pasadena City College, Pasadena, California

Financial Aid

Here are a few speech-language pathology-related scholarships. For more on financial aid for two-year students, turn to Appendix B.

The **Kathleen M. Peters Memorial Speech-Language Pathology Assistant Scholarship** goes to SLP-assistant students at Pasadena City College in Pasadena, California. http://www.pasadena.edu/slpa/scholarships.cfm

The **Vermont Speech-Language Hearing Association SLP-Assistant Scholarship** is awarded to students studying to become SLP-assistants. http://www.vslha.org/media/VSHAscholarshipAPP.pdf

Related Careers

Audiologist, occupational therapist, optometrist, physical therapist, recreational therapist, special education aide, and special education teacher.

Appendix A
Tools for Career Success

When 20-year-old Justin Schulman started job-hunting for a position as a fitness trainer—his first step toward managing a fitness facility—he didn't mess around. "I immediately opened the Yellow Pages and started calling every number listed under health and fitness, inquiring about available positions," he recalls. Schulman's energy and enterprise paid off: He wound up with interviews that led to several offers of part-time work.

Schulman's experience highlights an essential lesson for jobseekers: There are plenty of opportunities out there, but jobs won't come to you—especially the career-oriented, well-paying ones that that you'll want to stick with over time. You've got to seek them out.

Uncover Your Interests

Whether you're in high school or bringing home a full-time paycheck, the first step toward landing your ideal job is assessing your interests. You need to figure out what makes you tick. After all, there is a far greater chance that you'll enjoy and succeed in a career that taps into your passions, inclinations, and natural abilities. That's what happened with career-changer Scott Rolfe. He was already 26 when he realized he no longer wanted to work in the food industry. "I'm an avid outdoorsman," Rolfe says, "and I have an appreciation for natural resources that many people take for granted." Rolfe turned his passions into his ideal job as a forest technician.

If you have a general idea of what your interests are, you're far ahead of the game. You may know that you're cut out for a health care career, for instance, or one in business. You can use a specific volume of *Top Careers in Two Years* to discover what position to target. If you are unsure of your direction, check out the whole range of volumes to see the scope of jobs available. Ask yourself, what job or jobs would I most like to do if I *already* had the training and skills? Then remind yourself that this is what your two-year training will accomplish.

You can also use interest inventories and skills-assessment programs to further pinpoint your ideal career. Your school or public librarian or guidance counselor should be able to help you locate such assessments. Web sites such as America's Career InfoNet (http://www.acinet.org) and JobWeb (http://www.jobweb.com) also offer interest inventories. Don't forget the help advisers at any two-year college can provide to target your interests.

You'll find suggestions for Web sites related to specific careers at the end of each chapter in any *Top Careers in Two Years* volume.

Unlock Your Network

The next stop toward landing the perfect job is networking. The word may make you cringe. But networking isn't about putting on a suit, walking into a roomful of strangers, and pressing your business card on everyone. Networking is simply introducing yourself and exchanging job-related and other information that may prove helpful to one or both of you. That's what Susan Tinker-Muller did. Quite a few years ago, she struck up a conversation with a fellow passenger on her commuter train. Little did she know that the natural interest she expressed in the woman's accounts payable department would lead to news about a job opening there. Tinker-Muller's networking landed her an entry-level position in accounts payable with MTV Networks. She is now the accounts payable administrator.

Tinker-Muller's experience illustrates why networking is so important. Fully 80 percent of openings are *never* advertised, and more than half of all employees land their jobs through networking, according to the U.S. Bureau of Labor Statistics. That's 8 out of 10 jobs that you'll miss if you don't get out there and talk with people. And don't think you can bypass face-to-face conversations by posting your résumé on job sites like Monster.com and Hotjobs.com and then waiting for employers to contact you. That's so mid-1990s! Back then, tens of thousands, if not millions, of job seekers diligently posted their résumés on scores of sites. Then they sat back and waited . . . and waited . . . and waited. You get the idea. Big job sites like Monster and Hotjobs have their place, of course, but relying solely on an Internet job search is about as effective as throwing your résumé into a black hole.

Begin your networking efforts by making a list of people to talk to: teachers, classmates (and their parents), anyone you've worked with, neighbors, worship acquaintances, and anyone you've interned or volunteered with. You can also expand your networking opportunities through the student sections of industry associations (listed at the end of each chapter of *Top Careers in Two Years*); attending or volunteering at industry events, association conferences, career fairs; and through job-shadowing. Keep in mind that only rarely will any of the people on your list be in a position to offer you a job. But whether they know it or not, they probably know someone who knows someone who is. That's why your networking goal is not to ask for a job but the name of someone to talk with. Even when you network with an employer, it's wise to say something like, "You may not have any positions available, but might you know someone I could talk with to find out more about what it's like to work in this field?"

Also, keep in mind that networking is a two-way street. For instance, you may be talking with someone who has a job opening that isn't appropriate for you. If you can refer someone else to the employer, either person may well be disposed to help you someday in the future.

Dial-Up Help

Call your contacts directly, rather than e-mail them. (E-mails are too easy for busy people to ignore, even if they don't mean to.) Explain that you're a recent graduate in your field; that Mr. Jones referred you; and that you're wondering if you could stop by for 10 or 15 minutes at your contact's convenience to find out a little more about how the industry works. If you leave this message as a voicemail, note that you'll call back in a few days to follow up. If you reach your contact directly, expect that they'll say they're too busy at the moment to see you. Ask, "Would you mind if I check back in a couple of weeks?" Then jot down a note in your date book or set up a reminder in your computer calendar and call back when it's time. (Repeat this above scenario as needed, until you get a meeting.)

Once you have arranged to talk with someone in person, prep yourself. Scour industry publications for insightful articles; having up-to-date knowledge about industry trends shows your networking contacts that you're dedicated and focused. Then pull together questions about specific employers and suggestions that will set you apart from the job-hunting pack in your field. The more specific your questions (for instance, about one type of certification versus another), the more likely your contact will see you as an "insider," worthy of passing along to a potential employer. At the end of any networking meeting, ask for the name of someone else who might be able to help you further target your search.

Get a Lift

When you meet with a contact in person (as well as when you run into someone fleetingly), you need an "elevator speech." This is a summary of up to two minutes that introduces who you are, as well as your experience and goals. An elevator speech should be short enough to be delivered during an elevator ride with a potential employer from the ground level to a high floor. In it, it's helpful to show that 1) you know the business involved; 2) you know the company; 3) you're qualified (give your work and educational information); and 4) you're goal-oriented, dependable, and hardworking. You'll be surprised how much information you can include in two minutes. Practice this speech in front of a mirror until you have the key points down very well. It should sound natural though, and you should come across as friendly, confident, and assertive. Remember, good eye contact needs to be part of your presentation as well as your everyday approach when meeting prospective employers or leads.

Get Your Résumé Ready

In addition to your elevator speech, another essential job-hunting tool is your résumé. Basically, a résumé is a little snapshot of you in words, reduced to one 8½ x 11-inch sheet of paper (or, at most, two sheets). You need a résumé whether you're in high school, college, or the workforce, and whether you've never held a job or have had many.

At the top of your résumé should be your heading. This is your name, address, phone numbers, and your e-mail address, which can be a sticking point. E-mail addresses such as sillygirl@yahoo.com or drinkingbuddy @hotmail.com won't score you any points. In fact they're a turn-off. So if you dreamed up your address after a night on the town, maybe it's time to upgrade. (Similarly, these days potential employers often check Myspace sites, personal blogs, and Web pages. What's posted there has been known to cost candidates a job offer.)

The first section of your résumé is a concise Job Objective (e.g., "Entry-level agribusiness sales representative seeking a position with a leading dairy cooperative"). These days, with word-processing software, it's easy and smart to adapt your job objective to the position for which you're applying. An alternative way to start a résumé, which some recruiters prefer, is to re-work the Job Objective into a Professional Summary. A Professional Summary doesn't mention the position you're seeking, but instead focuses on your job strengths (e.g., "Entry-level agribusiness sales rep; strengths include background in feed, fertilizer, and related markets and ability to contribute as a member of a sales team"). Which is better? It's your call.

The body of a résumé typically starts with your Job Experience. This is a chronological list of the positions you've held (particularly the ones that will help you land the job you want). Remember: never, never any fudging. However, it is okay to include volunteer positions and internships on the chronological list, as long as they're noted for what they are.

Next comes your Education section. Note: It's acceptable to flip the order of your Education and Job Experience sections if you're still in high school or have gone straight to college and don't have significant work experience. Summarize the major courses in your degree area, any certifications you've achieved, relevant computer knowledge, special seminars, or other school-related experience that will distinguish you. Include your grade average if it's more than 3.0. Don't worry if you haven't finished your degree. Simply write that you're currently enrolled in your program (if you are).

In addition to these elements, other sections may include professional organizations you belong to and any work-related achievements, awards, or recognition you've received. Also, you can have a section for your interests, such as playing piano or soccer (and include any notable achievements regarding your interests, for instance, placed third in Midwest Regional Piano Competition). You should also note other special abilities, such as

"Fluent in French" or "Designed own Web site." These sorts of activities will reflect well on you, whether or not they are job-related.

You can either include your references or simply note, "References upon Request." Be sure to ask your references permission to use their name and alert them to the fact that they may be contacted, before you include them on your résumé. For more information on résumé writing, check out Web sites such as http://www.resume.monster.com.

Craft Your Cover Letter

When you apply for a job either online or by mail, it's appropriate to include a cover letter. A cover letter lets you convey extra information about yourself that doesn't fit or isn't always appropriate in your résumé. For instance, in a cover letter, you can and should mention the name of anyone who referred you to the job. You can go into some detail about the reason you're a great match, given the job description. You also can address any questions that might be raised in the potential employer's mind (for instance, a gap in your résumé). Don't, however, ramble on. Your cover letter should stay focused on your goal: to offer a strong, positive impression of yourself and persuade the hiring manager that you're worth an interview. Your cover letter gives you a chance to stand out from the other applicants and sell yourself. In fact, 23 percent of hiring managers say a candidate's ability to relate his or her experience to the job at hand is a top hiring consideration, according to a Careerbuilder.com survey.

You can write a positive, yet concise cover letter in three paragraphs: An introduction containing the specifics of the job you're applying for; a summary of why you're a good fit for the position and what you can do for the company; and a closing with a request for an interview, contact information, and thanks. Remember to vary the structure and tone of your cover letter. For instance, don't begin every sentence with "I."

Ace Your Interview

Preparation is the key to acing any job interview. This starts with researching the company or organization you're interviewing with. Start with the firm, group, or agency's own Web site. Explore it thoroughly; read about their products and services, their history, and sales and marketing information. Check out their news releases, links that they provide, and read up on or Google members of the management team to get an idea of what they may be looking for in their employees.

Sites such as http://www.hoovers.com enable you to research companies across many industries. Trade publications in any industry (such as *Food Industry News, Hotel Business,* and *Hospitality Technology*) are also available online or in hard copy at many college or public libraries. Don't forget to make a phone call to contacts you have in the organization to get an even better idea of the company culture.

Preparation goes beyond research, however. It includes practicing answers to common interview questions:

☞ *Tell me about yourself* (Don't talk about your favorite bands or your personal history; give a brief summary of your background and interest in the particular job area.)

☞ *Why do you want to work here?* (Here's where your research into the company comes into play; talk about the firm's strengths and products or services.)

☞ *Why should we hire you?* (Now is your chance to sell yourself as a dependable, trustworthy, effective employee.)

☞ *Why did you leave your last job?* (This is not a talk show. Keep your answer short; never bad-mouth a previous employer. You can always say something simply such as, "It wasn't a good fit, and I was ready for other opportunities.")

Rehearse your answers, but don't try to memorize them. Responses that are natural and spontaneous come across better. Trying to memorize exactly what you want to say is likely to both trip you up and make you sound robotic.

As for the actual interview, to break the ice, offer a few pleasant remarks about the day, a photo in the interviewer's office, or something else similar. Then, once the interview gets going, listen closely and answer the questions you're asked, versus making any other point that you want to convey. If you're unsure whether your answer was adequate, simply ask, "Did that answer the question?" Show respect, good energy, and enthusiasm, and be upbeat. Employers are looking for people who are enjoyable to be around, as well as good workers. Show that you have a positive attitude and can get along well with others by not bragging during the interview, overstating your experience, or giving the appearance of being too self-absorbed. Avoid one-word answers, but at the same time don't blather. If you're faced with a silence after giving your response, pause for a few seconds, and then ask, "Is there anything else you'd like me to add?" Never look at your watch or answer your cellphone during an interview.

Near the interview's end, the interviewer is likely to ask you if you have any questions. Make sure that you have a few prepared, for instance:

☞ *"Tell me about the production process."*

☞ *"What's your biggest short-term challenge?"*

☞ *"How have recent business trends affected the company?"*

☞ *"Is there anything else that I can provide you with to help you make your decision?"*

☞ *"When will you make your hiring decision?"*

During a first interview, never ask questions like, "What's the pay?" "What are the benefits?" or "How much vacation time will I get?"

Find the Right Look

Appropriate dressing and grooming is also essential to interviewing success. For business jobs and many other occupations, it's appropriate to come to an interview in a nice (not stuffy) suit. However, different fields have various dress codes. In the music business, for instance, "business casual" reigns for many jobs. This is a slightly modified look, where slacks and a jacket are just fine for a guy, and a nice skirt and blouse and jacket or sweater are acceptable for a woman. Dressing overly "cool" will usually backfire.

In general, watch all of the basics from the shoes on up (no sneakers or sandals, and no overly high heels or short skirts for women). Also avoid attention-getting necklines, girls. Keep jewelry and other "bling" to a minimum. Tattoos and body jewelry are becoming more acceptable, but if you can take out piercings (other than in your ear), you're better off. Similarly, unusual hairstyles or colors may bias an employer against you, rightly or wrongly. Make sure your hair is neat and acceptable (get a haircut?). Also go light on the makeup, self-tanning products, body scents, and other grooming agents. Don't wear a baseball cap or any other type of hat; and by all means, take off your sunglasses!

Beyond your physical appearance, you already know to be well bathed to minimize odor (leave your home early if you tend to sweat, so you can cool off in private), make good eye contact, smile, speak clearly using proper English, use good posture (don't slouch), offer a firm handshake, and arrive within five minutes of your interview. (If you're unsure of where you're going, "Mapquest" it and consider making a dry-run to the site so you won't be late.) First impressions can make or break your interview.

Remember Follow-Up

After your interview, send a thank you note. This thoughtful gesture will separate you from most of the other candidates. It demonstrates your ability to follow through, and it catches your prospective employer's attention one more time. In a 2005 Careerbuilder.com survey, nearly 15 percent of 650 hiring managers said they wouldn't hire someone who failed to send a thank you letter after the interview. Thirty-two percent say they would still consider the candidate, but would think less of him or her.

So do you hand write or e-mail the thank you letter? The fact is that format preferences vary. One in four hiring managers prefer to receive a thank you note in e-mail form only; 19 percent want the e-mail, followed up with a hard copy; 21 percent want a typed hard-copy only; and 23 percent prefer just a handwritten note. (Try to check with an assistant on the format your potential employer prefers.) Otherwise, sending an e-mail and a handwritten copy is a safe way to proceed.

Winning an Offer

There are no sweeter words to a job hunter than, "We'd like to hire you." So naturally, when you hear them, you may be tempted to jump at the offer. *Don't.* Once an employer wants you, he or she will usually give you some time to make your decision and get any questions you may have answered. Now is the time to get specific about salary and benefits, and negotiate some of these points. If you haven't already done so, check out salary ranges for your position and area of the country on sites such as Payscale.com, Salary.com, and Salaryexpert.com (basic info is free; specific requests are not). Also, find out what sorts of benefits similar jobs offer. Then don't be afraid to negotiate in a diplomatic way. Asking for better terms is reasonable and expected. You may worry that asking the employer to bump up his offer may jeopardize your job, but handled intelligently, negotiating for yourself in fact may be a way to impress your future employer—and get a better deal for yourself.

After you've done all the hard work that successful job-hunting requires, you may be tempted to put your initiative into autodrive. However, the efforts you made to land your job-from clear communication to enthusiasm-are necessary now to pave your way to continued success. As Danielle Little, a human-resources assistant, says, "You must be enthusiastic and take the initiative. There is an urgency to prove yourself and show that you are capable of performing any and all related tasks. If your manager notices that you have potential, you will be given additional responsibilities, which will help advance your career." So do your best work on the job, and build your credibility. Your payoff will be career advancement and increased earnings.

Appendix B

Financial Aid

One major advantage of earning a two-year degree is that it is much less expensive than paying for a four-year school. Two years is naturally going to cost less than four, and two-year graduates enter the workplace and start earning a paycheck sooner than their four-year counterparts.

The latest statistics from the College Board show that average yearly total tuition and fees at a public two-year college is $2,191, compared to $5,491 at a four-year public college. That cost leaps to more than $21,000 on average for a year at a private four-year school.

With college costs relatively low, some two-year students overlook the idea of applying for financial aid at all. But the fact is, college dollars are available whether you're going to a trade school, community college, or university. About a third of all Pell Grants go to two-year public school students, and while two-year students receive a much smaller percentage of other aid programs, the funding is there for many who apply.

How Does Aid Work?

Financial aid comes in two basic forms: merit-based and need-based.

Merit-based awards are typically funds that recognize a particular talent or quality you may have, and they are given by private organizations, colleges, and the government. Merit-based awards range from scholarships for good writing to prizes for those who have shown promise in engineering. There are thousands of scholarships available for students who shine in academics, music, art, science, and more. Resources on how to get these awards are provided later in this chapter.

Need-based awards are given according to your ability to pay for college. In general, students from families that have less income and fewer assets receive more financial aid. To decide how much of this aid you qualify for, schools look at your family's income, assets, and other information regarding your finances. You provide this information on a financial aid form—usually the federal government's Free Application for Federal Student Aid (FAFSA). Based on the financial details you provide, the school of your choice calculates your Expected Family Contribution (EFC). This is the amount you are expected to pay toward your education each year.

Once your EFC is determined, a school uses this simple formula to figure out your financial aid package:

Cost of attendance at the school

– Your EFC

– **Other outside aid (private scholarships)**

= Need

Schools put together aid packages that meet that need using loans,
work-study, and grants.

Know Your School

When applying to a school, it's a good idea to find out their financial aid
policy and history. Read over the school literature or contact the financial
aid office and find out the following:

✔ *Is the school accredited?* Schools that are not accredited usually do not
   offer as much financial aid and are not eligible for federal programs.

✔ *What is the average financial aid package at the school?* The typical award
   size may influence your decision to apply or not.

✔ *What are all the types of assistance available?* Check if the school offers
   federal, state, private, or institutional aid.

✔ *What is the school's loan default rate?* The default rate is the percentage
   of students who took out federal student loans and failed to repay
   them on time. Schools that have a high default rate are often not al-
   lowed to offer certain federal aid programs.

✔ *What are the procedures and deadlines for submitting financial aid?* Poli-
   cies can differ from school to school.

✔ *What is the school's definition of satisfactory academic progress?* To receive
   financial aid, you have to maintain your academic performance. A
   school may specify that you keep up at least a C+ or B average to keep
   getting funding.

✔ *What is the school's job placement rate?* The job placement rate is the
   percentage of students who find work in their field of study after
   graduating.

You'll want a school with a good placement rate so you can earn a good
salary that may help you pay back any student loans you have.

Be In It to Win It

The key to getting the most financial aid possible is filling out the forms, and you have nothing to lose by applying. Most schools require that you file the FAFSA, which is *free* to submit, and you can even do it online. For more information on the FAFSA, visit the Web site at http://www.fafsa.ed.gov. If you have any trouble with the form, you can call 1-800-4-FED-AID for help.

To receive aid using the FAFSA, you must submit the form soon after January 1 prior to the start of your school year. A lot of financial aid is delivered on a first-come, first-served basis, so be sure to apply on time.

Filing for aid will require some work to gather your financial information. You'll need details regarding your assets and from your income tax forms, which include the value of all your bank accounts and investments. The form also asks if you have other siblings in college, the age of your parents, or if you have children. These factors can determine how much aid you receive.

Three to four weeks after you submit the FAFSA, you receive a document called the Student Aid Report (SAR). The SAR lists all the information you provided in the FAFSA and tells you how much you'll be expected to contribute toward school, or your Expected Family Contribution (EFC). It's important to review the information on the SAR carefully and make any corrections right away. If there are errors on this document, it can affect how much financial aid you'll receive.

The Financial Aid Package

Using information on your SAR, the school of your choice calculates your need (as described earlier) and puts together a financial aid package. Aid packages are often built with a combination of loans, grants, and work-study. You may also have won private scholarships that will help reduce your costs.

Keep in mind that aid awarded in the form of loans has to be paid back with interest just like a car loan. If you don't pay back according to agreed upon terms, you can go into *default*. Default usually occurs if you've missed payments for 180 days. Defaulted loans are often sent to collection agencies, which can charge costly fees and even take money owed out of your wages. Even worse, a defaulted loan is a strike on your credit history. If you have a negative credit history, lenders may deny you a mortgage, car loan, or other personal loan. There's also financial incentive for paying back on time—many lenders will give a 1 percent discount or more for students who make consecutive timely payments. The key is not to borrow more than you can afford. Know exactly how much your monthly payments will be on a loan when it comes due and estimate if those monthly payments will fit in your future budget. If you ever do run into trouble with loan payments, don't hesitate to contact your lender and see if you can come up with a new payment arrangement—lenders want to help you pay rather than see you go into default. If you have more than one loan, look into loan consolidation, which can lower overall monthly payments and sometimes lock in interest rates that are relatively low.

The Four Major Sources of Aid

U.S. Government Financial Aid

The federal government is the biggest source of financial aid. To find all about federal aid programs, visit http://www.studentaid.fed.gov or call 1-800-4-FED-AID with any questions. Download the free brochure *Funding Education Beyond High School*, which tells you all the details on federal programs. To get aid from federal programs you must be a regular student working toward a degree or certificate in an eligible program. You also have to have a high school diploma or equivalent, be a U.S. citizen or eligible noncitizen and have a valid Social Security number (check http://www.ssa.gov for info). If you are a male aged 18–25, you have to register for the Selective Service. (Find out more about that requirement at http://www.sss.gov or call 1-847-688-6888.) You must also certify that you are not in default on a student loan and that you will use your federal aid only for educational purposes.

Some specifics concerning federal aid programs can change a little each year, but the major programs are listed here and the fundamentals stay the same from year to year. (Note that amounts you receive generally depend on your enrollment status—whether it be full-time or part-time.)

Pell Grant
For students demonstrating significant need, this award has been ranging between $400 and $4,050. The size of a Pell grant does not depend on how much other aid you receive.

Supplemental Educational Opportunity Grant (SEOG)
Again for students with significant need, this award ranges from $100 to $4,000 a year. The size of the SEOG can be reduced according to how much other aid you receive.

Work-Study
The Federal Work-Study Program provides jobs for students showing financial need. The program encourages community service and work related to a student's course of study. You earn at least minimum wage and are paid at least once a month. Again, funds must be used for educational expenses.

Perkins Loans
With a low interest rate of 5 percent, this program lets students who can document the need borrow up to $4,000 a year.

Stafford Loans
These loans are available to all students regardless of need. However, students with need receive *subsidized* Staffords, which do not accrue interest while you're in school or in deferment. Students without need can take *unsubsidized* Staffords, which do accrue interest while you are in school or in deferment. Interest rates vary but can go no higher than 8.25 percent. Loan amounts vary too, according to what year of study you're in and whether you are financially dependent on your parents or not. Students defined as independent of their parents can borrow much more. (Students who have their own kids are also defined as independent. Check the exact qualifications for independent and dependent status on the federal government Web site http://www.studentaid.fed.gov.)

PLUS Loans
These loans for parents of dependent students are also available regardless of need. Parents with good credit can borrow up to the cost of attendance minus any other aid received. Interest rates are variable but can go no higher than 9 percent.

Tax Credits
Depending on your family income, qualified students can take federal tax deductions for education with maximums ranging from $1,500 to $2,000.

AmeriCorps
This program provides full-time educational awards in return for community service work. You can work before, during, or after your postsecondary education and use the funds either to pay current educational expenses or to repay federal student loans. Americorps participants work assisting teachers in Head Start, helping on conservation projects, building houses for the homeless, and doing other good works. For more information, visit http://www.AmeriCorps.gov

State Financial Aid
All states offer financial aid, both merit-based and need-based. Most states use the FAFSA to determine eligibility, but you'll have to contact your state's higher education agency to find out the exact requirements. You can get contact information for your state at http://www.bcol02.ed.gov/Programs/

EROD/org_list.cfm. Most of the state aid programs are available only if you study at a school in the state where you reside. Some states are very generous, especially if you're attending a state college or university. California's Cal Grant program gives needy state residents free tuition at in-state public universities.

School-Sponsored Financial Aid

The school you attend may offer its own loans, grants, and work programs. Many have academic- or talent-based scholarships for top-performing students. Some two-year programs offer cooperative education opportunities where you combine classroom study with off-campus work related to your major. The work gives you hands-on experience and some income, ranging from $2,500 to $15,000 per year depending on the program. Communicate with your school's financial aid department and make sure you're applying for the most aid you can possibly get.

Private Scholarships

While scholarships for students heading to four-year schools may be more plentiful, there are awards for the two-year students. Scholarships reward students for all sorts of talent—academic, artistic, athletic, technical, scientific, and more. You have to invest time hunting for the awards that you might qualify for. The Internet now offers many great scholarship search services. Some of the best ones are:

The College Board (http://www.collegeboard.com/pay)
FastWeb! (http://www.fastweb.monster.com)
MACH25 (http://www.collegenet.com)
Scholarship Research Network (http://www.srnexpress.com)
SallieMae's College Answer (http://www.collegeanswer.com)

Note: Be careful of scholarship-scam services that charge a fee for finding you awards but end up giving you nothing more than a few leads that you could have gotten for free with a little research on your own. Check out the Federal Trade Commission's Project ScholarScam (http://www.ftc.gov/bcp/conline/edcams/scholarship).

In your hunt for scholarship dollars, be sure to look into local community organizations (the Elks Club, Lions Club, PTA, etc.), local corporations, employers (your employer or your parents' may offer tuition assistance), trade groups, professional associations (National Electrical Contractors Association, etc.), clubs (Boy Scouts, Girl Scouts, Distributive Education Club of America, etc.), heritage organizations (Italian, Japanese,

Chinese, and other groups related to ethnic origin), church groups, and minority assistance programs.

Once you find awards you qualify for, you have to put in the time applying. This usually means filling out an application, writing a personal statement, and gathering recommendations.

General Scholarships

A few general scholarships for students earning two-year degrees are

Coca-Cola Scholars Foundation, Inc.

Coca-Cola offers 350 thousand-dollar scholarships (http://www.coca colascholars.org) per year specifically for students attending two-year institutions.

Phi Theta Kappa (PTK)

This organization is the International Honor Society of the Two-Year College. PTK is one of the sponsors of the All-USA Academic Team program, which annually recognizes 60 outstanding two-year college students (http://scholarships.ptk.org). First, Second, and Third Teams, each consisting of 20 members, are selected. The 20 First Team members receive stipends of $2,500 each. All 60 members of the All-USA Academic Team and their colleges receive extensive national recognition through coverage in *USA TODAY*. There are other great scholarships for two-year students listed on this Web site.

Hispanic Scholarship Fund (HSF)

HSF's High School Scholarship Program (http://www.hsf.net/scholar ship/programs/hs.php) is designed to assist high school students of Hispanic heritage obtain a college degree. It is available to graduating high school seniors who plan to enroll full-time at a community college during the upcoming academic year. Award amounts range from $1,000 to $2,500.

The Military

All branches of the military offer tuition dollars in exchange for military service. You have to decide if military service is for you. The Web site http://www.myfuture.com attempts to answer any questions you might have about military service.

Lower Your Costs

In addition to getting financial aid, you can reduce college expenses by being a money-smart student. Here are some tips.

Use Your Campus

Schools offer perks that some students never take advantage of. Use the gym. Take in a school-supported concert or movie night. Attend meetings and lectures with free refreshments.

Flash Your Student ID

Students often get discounts at movies, museums, restaurants, and stores. Always be sure to ask if there is a lower price for students and carry your student ID with you at all times. You can often save 10 to 20 percent on purchases.

Budget Your Funds

Writing a budget of your income and expenses can help you be a smart spender. Track what you buy on a budget chart. This awareness will save you dollars.

Share Rides

Commuting to school or traveling back to your hometown? Check and post on student bulletin boards for ride shares.

Buy Used Books

Used textbooks can cost half as much as new. Check your campus bookstore for deals and also try http://www.eCampus.com and http://www.bookcentral.com

Put Your Credit Card in the Freezer

That's what one student did to stop overspending. You can lock your card away any way you like, just try living without the ease of credit for awhile. You'll be surprised at the savings.

A Two-Year Student's Financial Aid Package

Minnesota State Colleges and Universities provides this example of how a two-year student pays for college. Note how financial aid reduces his out-of-pocket cost to about $7,000 per year.

Jeremy's Costs for One Year

Jeremy is a freshman at a two-year college in the Minnesota. He has a sister in college, and his parents own a home but have no other significant savings. His family's income: $42,000.

College Costs for One Year

Tuition	$3,437
Fees	$388
Estimated room and board*	$7,200
Estimated living expenses**	$6,116
Total cost of attendance	$17,141

Jeremy's Financial Aid

Federal grants (does not require payment)	$2,800
Minnesota grant (does not require payment)	$676
Work-study earnings	$4,000
Student loan (requires repayment)	$2,625
Total financial aid	$10,101

Total cost to Jeremy's family	$7,040

* Estimated cost reflecting apartment rent rate and food costs. The estimates are used to calculate the financial aid. If a student lives at home with his or her parents, the actual cost could be much less, although the financial aid amounts may remain the same.

** This is an estimate of expenses including transportation, books, clothing, and social activities.

Index